# The Aid to Spain Movement in Battersea 1936–1939
By Mike Squires

With personal recollections
By Noreen Branson

© Mike Squires 1994

ISBN 0 9524029 0 4

Published by Elmfield Publications, 50 Elmfield Road, Balham, London SW17 8AL.
Printed by Lancashire Community Press (TU), 8 Higher Bank Road, Preston PR2 4PD.

Contents

Battersea – the Background	1
The Spanish Civil War 1936–1939	5
Battersea. The Origins of Aid to Spain	8
Aid to Spain Week 6–13th December 1936	11
The Battersea Ambulance	13
Post Ambulance activities on behalf of Aid to Spain	22
The Peace Council	26
How did Battersea's Aid to Spain movement compare with that of other areas?	29
Unity and Disunity	31
Fascism and Anti-Fascism	36
Defeat, and other battles	40
The Battersea Volunteers	44
List of the Battersea Volunteers	46
Short Biographies of the Battersea Volunteers	47
The Aid to Spain Movement in Battersea – The Transcript of a talk given by Noreen Branson	56
Notes	63

Acknowledgments

I should like to thank the following persons and institutions for their invaluable help with the production of this pamphlet.

Noreen Branson for first stimulating my interest in the topic. Harold Smith for both his comments on the original draft, and for his permission to photograph the Battersea ambulance plaque. Jim Fyrth, Bill Moore and Eddie Dare for their suggestions as to how the pamphlet could be improved. My thanks also to the Marx Memorial Library for allowing me to reproduce the articles from 'Volunteer for Liberty', which is contained in the Library's International Brigade Archive.

Battersea – the Background

The South London Borough of Battersea was situated between the River Thames to the North, Vauxhall to the East, Wandsworth to the West, and Clapham, Balham and Tooting to the South. The Borough was abolished in the Local Government reorganisation of 1964. It is now part of Wandsworth.

The Borough of Battersea was a mixture of solid working class areas in the northern part and some quite prosperous middle class neighbourhoods in the South. At the time of the outbreak of the Spanish Civil War in 1936, the Borough's two parliamentary divisions reflected this social division. Battersea North was held by the Labour MP, Stephen Sanders, and Battersea South, a more marginal seat, had elected a Tory MP, H.R. Selley. The Borough Council was Labour dominated and had been so, apart from two brief relapses, since the formation of the Battersea Trades and Labour Council in 1894.

The labour movement in Battersea was strong and well organised. Since the turn of the century it had played an influential role in the life of the Borough, and there was a large degree of interplay between the Trades and Labour Council and the local authority. Many of those who sat on the Borough Council as councillors, were also activists in the Trades Council, and numerous measures demanded by the Trades Council were implemented by the Borough Council. These included, alleviation of unemployment, a minimum wage for council employees, and the establishment of a Direct Works Department.

Until the middle of the First World War the Borough was run by an alliance of Labour councillors and Liberals. This alliance, know as the Progressives, dominated the Borough Council, and its predecessor the Vestry, from 1894 onwards. A split in the two groups occurred in 1915 over price increases, and from 1919 the council was run by a Labour administration. The Liberals faded away and played very little part in post First World War Battersea politics. The political terrain in Battersea, after 1918, was fought over between Labour and the Tories. Only once did the Conservatives win control of the Council, and that was in the exceptional year of 1931. Labour won back power in 1934 with a good majority and was in control of the Borough throughout the period of th e Spanish Civil War (1936–39).

Apart from local government, the Trades and Labour Council also exerted a decisive influence on the Borough's parliamentary representation. Battersea was represented in the House of Commons from 1894 until 1918 by John Burns, a charismatic and dominating figure in the local labour movement. Burns, supported by the local Liberals, and backed by his own creation, the Battersea Labour League, was Battersea's MP for 24 years. He declined to stand again in the Khaki election of 1918 and his successor Charlotte Despard, standing in the newly created Battersea North constituency, lost the seat. In Battersea South too Labour suffered a setback, and for a brief, and unique period, neither division returned a Labour MP. Three years later, with a new candidate, after Charlotte Despard's retirement to Ireland, Battersea North was won back for Labour. Labour's candidate at this election was another dynamic and influential labour movement figure, Shapurji Saklatvala.

Saklatvala, an Indian, who had moved to Britain in 1905, was an active, and well-known member of the newly created Communist Party of Great Britain. Between 1920, the year of the Party's formation, and 1924, communists could also be members of the Labour Party, there were no bans or proscriptions. Saklatvala like Burns before him, was to have a powerful effect on the Battersea Labour Party and Trades Council.

First elected in 1922, Saklatvala was defeated at the General Election of 1923, and re-elected in 1924, this time as a communist, but supported by the Battersea Labour Party and Trades Council. At the 1925 Annual Labour Party Conference, a decision was taken to exclude communists from the Labour Party. The Battersea Labour Party disagreed with the Conference decision and refused to implement the ban on communists. Saklatvala remained as the MP for Battersea North, until defeated by Stephen Sanders, the Labour candidate, in the General Election of 1929.

The divisions that Saklatvala's candidature aroused in the local labour movement were deep, and long lasting. The split between those who supported communist membership of the Labour Party, and those who were opposed, was to affect the work of the Battersea labour movement up until the Second World War. This split was also to figure, sometimes quite prominently, in the Aid to Spain movement in the Borough.

From the 1890s onwards Battersea politics was dominated by the local labour movement – it was a labour movement that had two distinct strands. One was its commitment to internationalism, and the other was its radicalism, of which the communists, after 1920, were seen as an essential part.

Internationalism showed itself early on in the life of Battersea's organised working class. Five years after the Trades Council's formation, the Boer war broke out in South Africa in 1899. The Battersea labour movement ranged itself unhesitatingly on the side of the Boers, who were fighting for an independent Boer state. Colonialism and aggressive nationalism found little response amongst Battersea's working class. A local Stop the War committee was established, which included members of the Trades Council. The Committee organised meetings and collections for the Boers. In a significant act of international solidarity two Boers were invited to put the Boer case at a packed meeting at Battersea Town Hall. Pro war meetings were taken over by anti war supporters, and no flags were flown on council property on Mafeking day – a day given over to celebrate the relief of the South African town of Mafeking which had been besieged by the Boers.

A few years later this internationalism showed itself again, when in 1905 the Borough Council sent a message of support to the Russian revolutionaries in their unsuccessful attempt to overthrow the Tsar. In addition to these actions, for many years Battersea Borough Council, unlike other local authorities, refused to give Battersea school children the day off to celebrate Empire day. There was no Union Jack flown over the Town Hall; instead the Council flew its own Municipal flag, with the socialist emblem, 'not for you, not for me, but for us'. This spirit of solidarity had much to do with the make-up of Battersea's labour movement. There was a strong Irish influence stemming from the Irish community based in the easterly end of the Borough. Beyond the Dogs Home Bridge by Nine Elms Lane, the area was known as 'Irish Island'. T. Brogan, a prominent member of the Irish community and an active nationalist, was elected the Mayor of the Borough in 1912. Until the Irish Treaty of 1921, the labour movement in its demand for colonial independence, usually linked Ireland with other colonies, particularly India. Brogan's successor as Mayor, John Archer, also added to the Borough's internationalist outlook. Archer, a Labour councillor and an activist in the Battersea labour movement until his death in 1932, was of mixed race. This proved no barrier to his rise to prominence locally. Apart from serving as Mayor, he was also for a time the secretary of the North Battersea Divisional Labour Party, and a member of the Borough Council for over twenty years.

This lack of chauvinism again asserted itself with the adoption of Shapurji Saklatvala as the Labour candidate in 1921. Saklatvala, through his activities in the Labour Party, the Independent Labour Party and the Workers Welfare League of India, had continually raised at national level the rights of nations to self determination. Saklatvala was an Indian, but that did not prevent him from gaining the unqualified support of the Battersea labour movement at three General Elections, 1922, 1923, and 1924. It was only after the labour movement split over the admissibility of communists to the Labour Party, that

Saklatvala was finally jettisoned as the parliamentary candidate of a united Battersea labour movement.

Although Saklatvala died in January 1936, six months before the Spanish Civil war broke out, his opponents and supporters in the Borough were still in conflict. The bitterness reflected the harsh struggle that had taken place throughout much of the twenties over the advisability of communist participation in the Labour Party. For a time there were even two Trades and Labour Councils in existence in the Borough, each vying with the other for members. One included communists, the other did not. The struggle was finally won by the opponents of the communists in 1928, helped to some degree by the communists own rejection of the Labour Party. But the legacy of this conflict lingered on years later, and was to effect the workings of the Aid to Spain movement in the area.

Apart from support for international causes, the Battersea labour movement had developed over the years in a revolutionary direction. There were a number of active socialist organisations in the borough from the time of John Burns onwards. The Social Democratic Federation had a branch in Battersea. The Borough was the birthplace of the Socialist Sunday School movement. Before the First World War there was a Battersea Socialist Council and a Battersea Socialist Party, both of which were active in the area. There was also a flourishing branch of the 'Daily Herald' League.

The effect of the Russian Revolution in 1917 on Battersea's working class movement was profound. Many Battersea Labour Party activists joined the newly formed Communist Party, after its foundation Congress in 1920. Amongst others, who did not join, there was widespread sympathy for the achievements of the Bolsheviks. From 1920 onwards there was organised communist activity in the locality, and the Battersea branch of the Communist Party soon won affiliation to the local Labour Party and Trades Council. In the early twenties a number a Labour councillors were also members of the Communist Party, and communists were accepted as an integral part of the Battersea labour movement.

Amongst all sections of Battersea's organised working class there was opposition to the rise of fascism. Within months of the Nazis coming to power in Germany in 1933, there was an anti-fascist meeting in the Borough. Saklatvala was one of the speakers at the meeting which was organised by the newly created Relief Committee for the Victims of German Fascism.

Given the Borough's radical and internationalist tradition it is not surprising that when the Spanish war broke out Battersea's working class responded in the way that they did. For over three years there were collections of food, money and supplies for the beleaguered Spanish Republic. Battersea people even contributed enough to send a fully equipped ambulance to help the Republican cause. This ambulance, with Battersea emblazoned on the side, helped ferry the Republic's wounded back from the battlefield to behind the front line. There were also a number of volunteers from Battersea who enrolled with the International Brigade. The Brigade was formed in December 1936 to help win recruits from all over the world for Spain's fight against fascism. A number of these men from Battersea who enlisted lost their lives.

The Spanish Civil War 1936–39

In February 1936, at the General Election, the people of Spain rejected their right wing rulers and elected a Popular Front Government. This Government was dominated by Liberal Republicans. It also consisted of some Socialists, and later a small number of Communists. Its moderate plans, which included land redistribution and democratic reform, were too much for the wealthy Spanish landowners. They, in conjunction with high ranking officers in the army, who were drawn from the same social class, began to plot against the government. General Franco, whose anti democratic views were well known, had been exiled to the Canary Islands to keep him out of the way. He had previously earned the animosity of large numbers of Spaniards for his role in suppressing the Asturias uprising in 1934. This revolt against the then extreme right wing, quasi fascist regime, was led by the Asturian miners. The rebellion was put down by Franco, with the loss of 1,500 dead, 3,000 wounded and 25,000 imprisoned.

In spite of his banishment from mainland Spain, on July 17th, 1936, Franco, and other army officers, staged a military revolt against the Government. The rebellion was quickly put down in most of the industrial areas. Here, unarmed workers and hastily mobilised workers militia, were successful in defeating the rebels. Only parts of the North of the country, and pockets in the South were retained by Franco. These were mainly economically disadvantaged, and poor rural areas. Thus the stage was set for a three year conflict, but as two participants and commentators on the Spanish war have observed, "if it had remained simply a Spanish war, there is little doubt that the Republican Government, supported by the Air Force and most of the Fleet, would have defeated the rebellion".[1]

Although it is usually referred to as a civil war, the war in Spain can be much more accurately described as a war by Germany and Italy on the Spanish people. The two fascist dictatorships used Spain, with the connivance of Franco

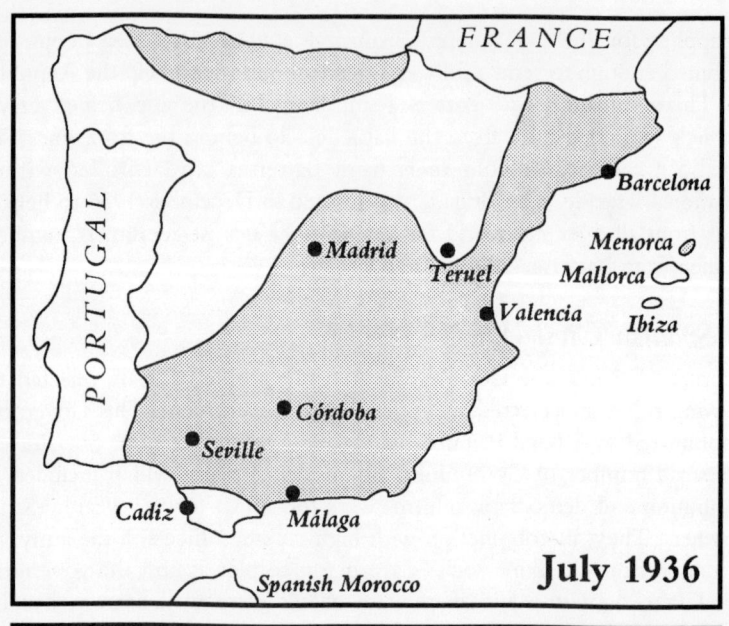

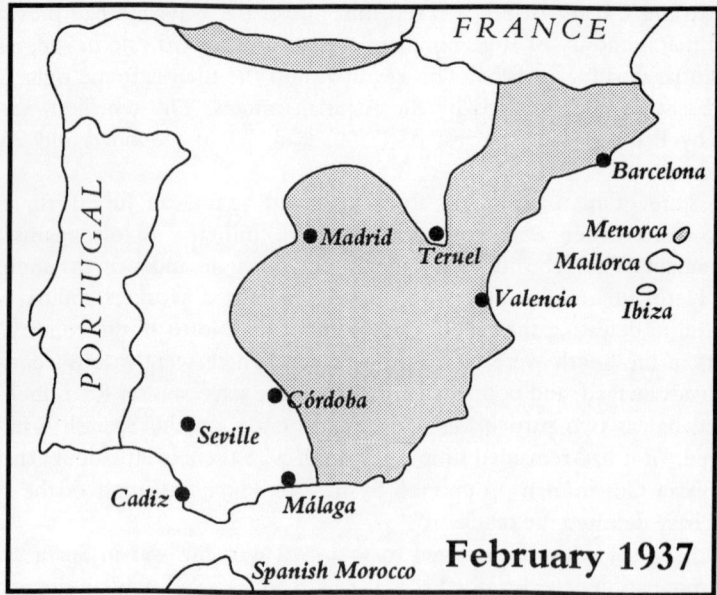

The Division of Spain, July 1936–July 1938

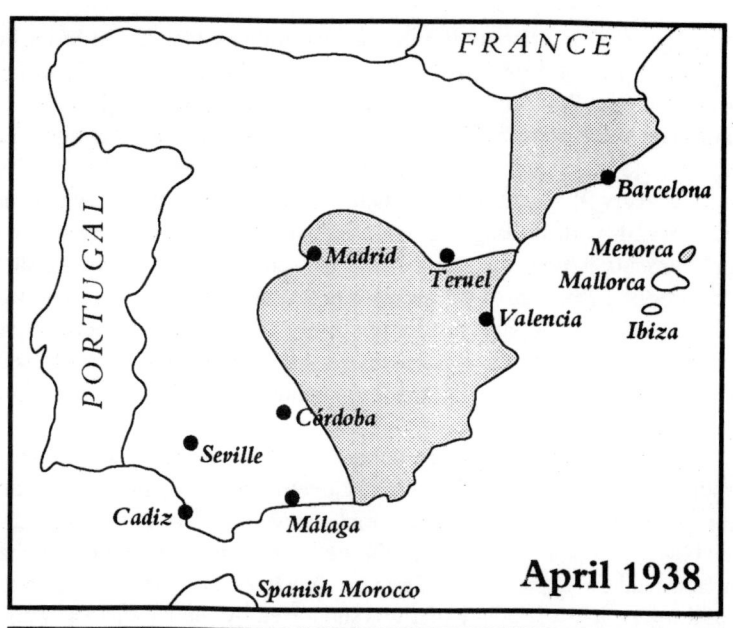

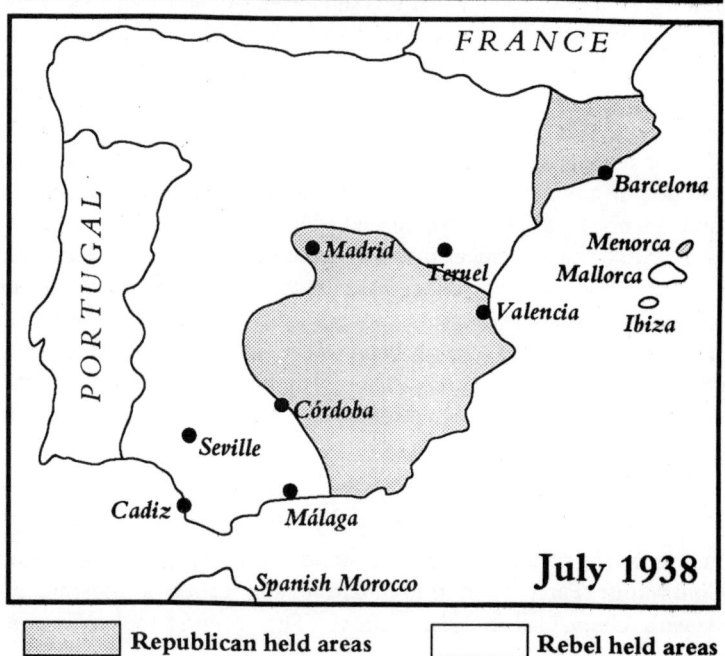

April 1938

July 1938

Republican held areas   Rebel held areas

and his supporters, as a testing ground for their military tactics. On Spanish soil, in Spanish airspace and on Spanish seas, many of the battles and skirmishes of the Second World War were given their first trial run. Italy sent 150,000 troops to Spain, and there were 5,318 Italian bombing raids on the Republic. Hitler despatched a Special Air Unit, plus anywhere between 20,000 and 50,000 troops. Germany also sent advisers, tank units and artillery to help Franco's forces. Portugal, with its long border with Spain, also provided invaluable help to the insurgents. Under the Dictatorship of General Salazar, Portugal allowed Franco's troops passage through the country, the use of Portuguese aerodromes and telecommunications, and in addition 15,000 Portuguese soldiers fought on Franco's side. Although The United States of America was officially neutral, that did not prevent Standard Oil from supplying Franco with petrol and oil on credit.

While the Spanish rebels were flooded with aid, troops, planes, munitions and supplies, the democratically elected Government of Spain was denied the right to buy arms. This policy of 'non-intervention' as it was called, was initiated by Britain and supported by the Popular Front Government in France. It was also paid lip service to by Germany and Italy. For the all important first year of the war, it was a policy that was supported by the Labour Party and the Trades Union Congress. It was not until a year later that the labour movement finally reversed this policy and supported Spain's right to purchase arms for its own defence.

Throughout the two and a half years of the Spanish conflict, the British Government remained adamant in its support of the non-intervention policy. This was despite a number of British merchant vessels trading with Spain being sunk by Franco's ships. Britain too turned a blind eye while Germany and Italy blatantly violated the agreement that they had signed. When the Republic was finally defeated, Britain, with undue haste, recognised Franco as the legitimate ruler of Spain, despite widespread protests from the labour movement. Six months after the defeat of Spanish democracy, Germany invaded Poland and Britain was finally forced to make a stand. The Second World War broke out and ultimately, in alliance with the USSR. and the USA., Britain at last confronted the fascist dictators.

Battersea. The Origins of Aid to Spain

Within two weeks of the start of the Spanish conflict, the Battersea branch of the Communist Party took the initiative and called a meeting at the railwaymen's Unity Hall in Falcon Grove. The meeting took place on July

31st, 1936, and was entitled, 'Support Spanish Workers against Fascism'. The main theme of the meeting, even at this early stage, was opposition to the policy of non-intervention. Tom Oldershaw, a Battersea communist, was the principal speaker. He was on a cycling holiday in Spain at the time of the revolt. He described to the audience his experiences, and particularly the poverty of places like Barcelona. He was none too flattering of Spain's commitment to hygiene, "there was apparently no laws to prevent the dumping of refuse in the Mediterranean – it smelt"[2] He was also prophetic in his assessment of the Spanish situation. He told his listeners, "the present situation in Spain must not be treated as just another internal revolution. The situation had all the makings of another world war".[3]

The other main speaker at the meeting was Clive Branson, another Battersea communist, who later went to Spain and was captured by the rebels. Clive Branson's wife, Noreen Branson, was the secretary of the Battersea branch of the Communist Party, which at that time had about 50 members.

It was the communists who first organised a public collection for the Spanish Government. In August, at one of their regular open air meetings at Comyn Road near Clapham Junction, the Battersea communists collected £1.0.6d.*

The meeting was presided over by Dan Lewis, the Communist Party organiser in Battersea, and other speakers included Bill Johnson, a Trades Council activist, and David Guest. Guest, the son of a Labour MP, had come to live in Battersea, and was later killed in Spain. The meeting was attended by 300 people and was described as 'enthusiastic and with no opposition'.[4]

It was the local branch of the Communist Party that hosted the first major public meeting in Battersea on Spain. Once again the theme was opposition to the Government policy of non-intervention. The meeting was held in the Battersea Town Hall on September 13th, 1936. It attracted over 400 people, and there was a collection of £13.10s.[5] Once again the local speakers were Dan Lewis and Clive Branson. J.R. Campbell, represented the Communist Party's Executive Committee, and another of the speakers was Ted Bramley from the London District Committee.

The Battersea communists continued their solidarity campaign with Spain, by calling another meeting at the Town Hall for November 1st. At this event Isabel Brown, one of the leaders of the newly established Medical Aid for Spain agreed to speak. Brown, a leading communist activist was noted for her

---

* Throughout the pamphlet wherever money is indicated, to appreciate the value in today's terms the reader is advised to multiply by 40. Thus, the first collection raised over £40, which was not bad for a street corner meeting in an area where many were unemployed.

tremendous oratory. In addition, the Labour MP Aneurin Bevan was approached to take part. Bevan, a prominent Labour left winger was opposed to the non-intervention policy. He agreed to participate, but suggested that it would be easier for him with the Labour Party leadership, if the meeting was not called by the Communist Party. The Battersea communists agreed to this, and the meeting was called under the auspices of an ad hoc Aid to Spain committee, which included several local trade union branches. The response to the meeting was overwhelming and staggered even the most optimistic. Over 1,000 people turned up and the Town Hall was packed to capacity. There was a collection of £35. Bevan warned the audience that, 'if Madrid fell to fascism, it would be Paris next, and then London'.[6]

By the time of the meeting, discussions were already taking place in the Battersea branch of the Communist Party about the advisability of establishing a broad Aid to Spain committee to include all those organisations in the borough in sympathy with the Republic. This move was given a further impetus by the success of the November 1st event. At a party branch meeting it was agreed that Communist Party members on the Battersea Trades Council would raise the issue of the establishment of an Aid to Spain committee.[7]

At the Trades Council meeting in November, Tom Oldershaw, a delegate from the Battersea Number 2 branch of the Amalgamated Society of Woodworkers seconded a resolution from the branch that a co-ordinating committee be established to facilitate aid to Spain. There was general agreement amongst the delegates about the need for help for Spain, but there was some discord about how this should be done. There was opposition to forming yet another separate committee, and instead the Trades council decided to establish a sub-committee, 'which would consider ways of helping Spain', and would have the power to co-opt members.[8]

This decision was ratified at the December meeting of the Trades Council, and it was agreed that the Aid to Spain sub-committee should consist of the following trades council delegates, Derwent, Wye, Oldershaw, Smith, Cadwell, Lewin and Fowler. Apart from Tom Oldershaw, Cadwell was also a member of the Communist Party.[9] The effect of the decision was that in future Aid to Spain would be organised directly by the Trades Council.

The initiative for such a venture had been taken by the local Communist Party. For the first three months of the Spanish war it was the Battersea communists that had campaigned single handed on behalf of the Republic. At this time both the TUC and the Labour Party supported the policy of non-intervention. The £35 that had been collected at the Town Hall meeting in November was handed over by the Battersea communists to the Trades Council.

Although there was now established a united Aid to Spain movement in the Borough, there was some overlap in the early stages between the work of the Trades Council and the Battersea Communist Party.

Aid To Spain Week 6–13th December 1936

An Aid to Spain week was first raised by the Battersea communists in November. It would consist of a week of activities and collections to help the Republic. In a letter to the Trades Council the local party branch made it clear that they did not wish to interfere with anything that the Trades Council may be doing about Spain.[10] At this stage the Trades Council had not yet formally established its Aid to Spain Committee. The Trades Council welcomed the communists' initiative and agreed that the proposed week did not conflict with anything that they had planned. However, the Trades Council declined to be represented at the events by a speaker. A motion from Ernest Perry, later the MP for Battersea South, in support of this was rejected, and instead the Trades Council agreed that participation in the week's activities should be left to individuals. It was an early indication of the hostility still felt towards the communists by some in the Battersea labour movement.

The Aid Spain Week took place from December 6–13th, 1936. Although the Trades Council declined to be officially represented it did notify all of its affiliated organisations about the week and asked them to help. The response of the Battersea Labour League of Youth was magnificent. In alliance with the Battersea branch of the Young Communist League the two organisations concentrated their efforts on collecting for the Spanish Youth Food Ship, which was due to leave for Spain on Christmas Eve.

Young communists and young socialists in Battersea leafleted many of the streets in the Borough appealing for tins of milk, sugar, or any kind of tinned food. They then took wheelbarrows up and down these streets and collected what they could. In the space of a week they had accumulated a massive amount of food. When the Food Ship left port, of the 93 tonnes of food on board one tonne had come from Battersea.

Apart from collections of foodstuffs, throughout the week money was collected for Spain at the Battersea Bus Garage. There was also carol singing to raise funds, and in a particularly novel, and publicity minded venture, a group of women knitted 60 garments for Spain. This was done in full public view. The women sat knitting in the window of the People's Bookshop at number 115, Lavender Hill. The People's Bookshop was run by the Communist Party, and had been established by David Guest.

The week concluded with a packed meeting on Spain at the Town Hall. Over twenty organisations were represented on the platform. These included 8 Trade Union branches, 2 Womens Co-op Guilds, Tenants Associations, 5 Labour Party wards, 2 Labour League of Youth branches, the Battersea Communist Party and the Battersea Young Communist League. The speakers included the leading left winger John Strachey, Langdon Davis from the 'News Chronicle', one of the few newspapers sympathetic to the Republic, and

Clothes for Spain's fighters are being knitted in the window of the People's Bookshop, Lavender Hill, Battersea.

Daily Worker, 12th December 1936.

Councillor Lewin, who was a member of the Battersea Borough Council. The meeting was chaired by Clive Branson from the Communist Party. The collection raised £55.[11] It was a fitting end to a week that had raised the profile of Spain amongst many in Battersea.

The Battersea Ambulance

It was David Guest that had the idea of sending an ambulance from Battersea to Spain. Councillor Wye, who was the Chairman of the Aid to Spain Committee, made clear that it was Guest, who at the first meeting of the committee in December 1936, made the suggestion of funding a Battersea ambulance.[12] Guest proposed that the money raised by the Communist Party at its November meeting, which had now been handed over to the Trades Council's Aid to Spain committee, be used as a basis for such a project. His proposal was accepted by the Trades Council and they began the huge task of collecting the necessary sum. It would cost £750 to equip and send an ambulance to Spain.

As a first step, the Trades Council issued and circulated an appeal, signed by the Mayor, and other people prominent in the Borough. This appeal asked for donations towards the cost of the ambulance. In addition the Aid to Spain committee organised a meeting in the Town Hall for Sunday, January 11th, 1937. The meeting was advertised under the slogan, 'Battersea Ambulance for Spain'. There was an array of speakers, including David Guest's sister, who spoke, according to the local paper, dressed in an artillery person's overcoat. She was already working in Spain for the Republican cause. Another of the speakers was McKinnon Wood, who was the Labour LCC candidate for Battersea South. He was also a member of the Committee of Inquiry of breaches of International law in Spain. Caroline Ganley, who was a long standing Labour Party activist in Battersea, and later the MP for Battersea South, was also on the platform. The meeting was chaired by Councillor Coles, and Dan Lewis from the Communist Party made the appeal. The meeting got the ambulance appeal off to a good start with a collection of over £40.[13]

David Guest, with his youthful enthusiasm, and commitment to the ambulance, decided that things needed to be speeded up. He went to the Spanish Medical Aid HQ in London and made arrangements for an ambulance to be sent to Spain. At that time, the beginning of 1937, only £100 out of the £750 had been collected towards the costs. He made a further visit to the Spanish Medical HQ in January, and finalised the arrangements. The Battersea ambulance was despatched for Spain and carried on its side a plate with the

A ton of food was collected in Battersea for Spain. A great quantity was brought to the Town Hall Meeting.

W.S. Sanders, M.P. for North Battersea and John Strachey (right), were among the speakers at the Battersea Town Hall Meeting for Spain.

Daily Worker, 15th December 1936.

inscription, "from the workers of Battersea to the defenders of democracy in Spain". According to Wye, David Guest was severely criticised by the local committee for his actions.[14] David Guest's response was that now that the ambulance had been sent it would act as a spur to raise the money. Ultimately the Trades Council did achieve this objective, but it was not until August 1938, some eighteen months later. Ironically it was within a month of David Guest's own death. He was killed in July 1938, fighting for the International Brigade in Spain.

The Aid to Spain Committee's campaign for the ambulance fund was marked by a mixture of success and failure. In March 1937, less than three months after the ambulance campaign had been launched, Wye reported to the Trades Council that £265 had been raised. This was over a third of the agreed sum. At this rate it would not take long to get the £750. However, by June 1937, there was some disquiet amongst certain trade unions affiliated to the Trades Council as to the success of the campaign. The Transport and General Workers Union, Battersea branch number 1/425, sent a resolution to the Trades Council urging, "an immediate campaign to find the balance of £250 required for the Battersea Ambulance to Spain".[15]

The T and G branch seem to have been badly misinformed about the amount of money raised. It was far less than the £500 that their resolution implied. At the Trades Council's AGM in February 1938, the treasurer told the delegates that they had still only raised £430 towards the ambulance. But by April 1938, things had picked up and Wye reported to the monthly Trades council meeting that they were only £43 short of their £750 target. He also complimented the work done by a group of Aid to Spain supporters at the Dorman Long factory, which to date had sent in £100 for Spanish aid.

The sub-committee organised a whole series of events and activities on behalf of the ambulance fund. Apart from the regular collections at Dorman Long's, there were also collections at Battersea Bus Garage. There were talent contests, dances, whist drives. A dance in April, 1938 raised £4.10 and a whist Drive £3. Small amounts but they all helped.[16] A Swimming Gala was arranged at the Latchmere Baths in September 1937, at which a large number of local teams took part. A particularly successful event was a fete at the Battersea Stadium in Lombard Road on July 7th–9th, 1938. The Stadium was given free of charge, and all trade union branches affiliated to the Trades Council were urged to give their maximum support. It was quite an ambitious programme. The Spanish Ambassador was to attend but had to decline at the last moment due to another engagement. There were boxing matches refereed by George Adams, a well-known Battersea boxer. There was a women's egg and spoon

BAZAAR & FUN FAIR
TO HELP THE AMBULANCE TO SPAIN
— AT —
BATTERSEA (Grand) TOWN HALL
TUESDAY, FEBRUARY 23, at 3 p.m.

OPENER—
MRS. SAKLATVALA

GAY STALLS, FUN FAIR, BOOKS, etc.
DANCING from 8 p.m. to 11.30
SPANISH CABARET
Admission 6d.
COME AND HAVE A JOLLY DAY.

SAVE LONDON AND MADRID FROM FASCISM AND TORYISM

Communist Youth Rally
BATTERSEA TOWN HALL
(LOWER)
Sunday, February 21, 7.30 p.m.

PLAY—
"WHO ARE THE ENGLISH"

Speakers: JOHN GOLLAN, DAVE GUEST, and SAM MASTERS, recently returned from Spain.
ADMISSION FREE.

South Western Star, 19th February, 1937.

race. A 'strong man', John Callaghan, according to the South Western Star, "treated bars of iron like biscuits".[17] There was music from the South West Area Young Communist League Bugle band, and a dancing display by Basque children, who had recently come to Britain from Spain. The fete raised over £27, and with it the ambulance appeal surpassed the £750 target.

The first driver of the Battersea ambulance was Percy Cohen. In November 1937, it was announced by the Spanish Medical Aid Committee that Cohen was back in England, having been given a few days leave. With Cohen's agreement, the Battersea Aid Spain Committee utilised his services to help with their ambulance fund raising. Cohen attended a social organised by the South Battersea Divisional Labour Party, and spoke about his experiences in Spain.[18] After Percy Cohen, Joe Ilean became the driver of the Battersea ambulance. The changeover occurred sometime in 1938. There seems to have been only two drivers of the ambulance throughout its service in Spain.

The campaign for the Battersea Ambulance involved not just the Trades Council's Aid to Spain Committee, but other organisations as well. The Battersea Communist Party, despite initiating the aid Spain movement locally, continued with its own campaign to raise ambulance funds. The Battersea Young Communist League held a youth rally at the Town Hall in February 1937. The event was organised under the slogan, 'Save London and Madrid from Fascism and Toryism'. The speakers included John Gollan, the National Secretary of the Young Communist League, and David Guest. To add some culture to the proceedings there was also a play, 'Who are the English' by J. Lindsay. The meeting was free, but there was a collection on behalf of the ambulance fund.[19] In the previous month the Battersea Young Communists had organised a joint venture with the local Labour League of Youth branch. The big attractions of this meeting were a film, 'The Defence of Madrid', plus the two leaders of the Young Communist League and the Labour League of Youth, John Gollan and Ted Willis.[20]

As part of the Communist Party's campaign to win seats on the London County Council, the Battersea branch organised a joint LCC/Spain meeting. Harry Pollitt, the party's General Secretary, spoke in the Large Hall at the Latchmere Baths in February 1937. Once again the collection was on behalf of the ambulance. Although at the meeting Pollitt called for unity in the face of fascism, he was none too sympathetic to Battersea's Borough Council's efforts to publicise the forthcoming royal coronation. Pollitt told the audience, "there are thousands of workers who will be kidded again into painting the pavements red, white and blue for the coronation, like they did at the jubilee".[21] This was a reference to the Borough Council's decision to establish a special Coronation

No. 1704

BATTERSEA BOROUGH LABOUR PARTY AND TRADES COUNCIL AID SPAIN COMMITTEE

Grand Fete and Funfair

to be held at

THE BATTERSEA STADIUM
(By kind permission of Mr. Arden, "The White Hart")
LOMBARD ROAD, S.W.11

on

THURSDAY, FRIDAY & SATURDAY
7th, 8th and 9th JULY, 1938

OPENING CEREMONY

by His Excellency THE SPANISH AMBASSADOR

ADMISSION BY PROGRAMME EACH DAY **THREEPENCE**

ALL PROCEEDS TO AID SPAIN

● Purchase of Programme includes participation in grand Free Prize Distribution

• SHOWS • FORTUNE TELLING • < And all around you > • AUNT SALLY • ROUNDABOUTS •

THURSDAY, 7th JULY *Doors open 6 o'clock*

GREAT SEARCH FOR MICROPHONE TALENT!
CAN YOU SING, MIMIC, PLAY AN INSTRUMENT?
All May Enter
Entries before Monday, 4th July, to NAOMIE DIX, 52 Altenburg Gardens, S.W.11

SPECIAL LADIES' ANKLE COMPETITION
Entry Fee 2d. on ground   "The Shape of Things To Come"

COMMUNITY SINGING   "Memories in Music"

SPECIAL SURPRISE ITEM ? ? ? ? ?

SKIPPING COMPETITION FOR MEN, WOMEN AND CHILDREN

FRIDAY, 8th JULY *Doors open 6 o'clock*

GRAND EXHIBITION BOXING MATCHES
Three 2-minute Rounds at 3 stone

BILL HEARN v. TED MORRIS
both of South London and Real Champions
by courtesy of Syd Hearn, Esq.

CHILDREN'S BALLOON BURSTING COMPETITION
Entry Fee 1d. on ground   "A Good Bancoot"

SPECIAL ATTRACTION !!!
BATTERSEA'S STRONG MAN — JOHN CALLAGHAN
"Treats Bars of Iron Like Biscuits"

DANCING EVERY EVENING TO "THE ACCORDIONISTS"

SATURDAY, 9th JULY *Doors open 2 o'clock*

GRAND SPORTS DAY

CHILDREN'S RACES 100 YARDS HANDICAP
Boys 8-14 years   Girls 8 to 14 years
Entry fee 1d. on ground

ADULT RACES — LADIES' EGG AND SPOON RACE
MEN'S SACK RACE   VETERANS RACE (Men over 40)
Entry Fee 2d. on ground

GRAND CATCH WEIGHT TUG-OF-WAR CHALLENGE
TEAMS OF EIGHT TO COMPETE
Entries from T.U. Branches, L.O.Y.s, Y.C.L.s and Labour Party Ward Branches, not later than 7th July to
W. PRITCHARD, 115 Lavender Hill, S.W.11
Entry Fee 5/- per Team

BASQUE CHILD REFUGEES
Grand Dancing Display

SOUTH-WEST AREA BUGLE BAND

DONKEY DERBY

• RELAYED MUSIC ALL THE TIME
• MANY VALUABLE PRIZES GIVEN AWAY
• < And all around you > •

• WHEEL-'EM-IN • COMPETITIONS • ROLLING HORSE • HOUP-LA •

Committee. The committee had recommended that municipal buildings be decorated to celebrate the event, school children be given a special memento, and the borough's old people be provided with a coronation tea and entertainment. It was a far cry from the days in the not so distant past when Battersea's municipal Labour leaders would have nothing to do with royalty, or pomp or circumstance. Battersea republicanism, once such a novel feature in the Borough, was now at a low ebb.[22]

The Battersea communists throughout 1937 organised a number of public meetings at which money was raised for the ambulance. One such meeting in April 1937 was advertised as a, 'public welcome to the leader of the Saklatvala Unit of the International Brigade'.[23] It referred to Dave Springhall, who had been wounded at the defence of Madrid. The title Saklatvala Unit, named after Battersea's ex MP, had a very short life. The name was never widely accepted in Spain and by the middle of 1937 it had fallen into disuse.

In order to gain maximum publicity for the ambulance fund, at the People's Bookshop on Lavender Hill, a large placard with a map painted on it was placed above the window. The map showed the route from London to Madrid. Every time £50 was raised towards the goal of £750, a toy ambulance was moved farther along the London Madrid road.

The North Battersea Women's Co-op Guild also played a vital role in collecting money for the ambulance. In February 1937, the Guild organised a major fund raising event – a bazaar and cabaret at the Battersea Town Hall. The bazaar was opened by Mrs Saklatvala, and was given extensive coverage by the local paper. The paper's report gave something of the flavour of Aid to Spain events (see page 21).[24]

The North Battersea Women's Co-op Guild, which made regular collections on behalf of Spain, could attract large numbers of people to its events. At a concert in the Latchmere Baths in October 1938, there were over 600 in the audience.[25] At a Children's party organised by the Guild in the Town Hall, in January 1938, 350 children were in attendance. A representative of the Spanish Embassy was present, and the Mayor of Battersea made an appearance. There were dancing displays by members of the Battersea Co-operative dancing classes, and a theatrical sketch by members of the East Hill Baptist Church. Mrs Varran, an active Guildswomen, who had helped organise the party, had got donations from the local branch of Marks and Spencer and the Metropolitan Chain Stores, both situated in St. John's Road, near Clapham Junction.[26]

This huge poster, advertising Battersea's campaign to send an Ambulance to Spain, dominates the main road from its position above the People's Bookshop. A little Ambulance, moved along the road as the money is collected, has already reached Paris— a third of the way to success.

Daily Worker, 14th January, 1937.

Post Ambulance activities on behalf of Aid to Spain

At the Trades Council's Aid to Spain sub-committee meeting in August 1938, the treasurer Wye, reported that the Ambulance appeal had now surpassed its £750 target by £20. Ned Skinner, who at the same meeting resigned as the secretary of the sub-committee, suggested that the fund raising should continue. He proposed that in future all money collected should be divided in three parts. One part be given to the Basque Children's Fund,[27] another to the International

BATTERSEA AMBULANCE FOR SPAIN

Bazaar and Cabaret at the Town Hall

Bold chalkings on Tuesday afternoon indicated that all roads led to Battersea Town Hall, and that that building was in direct association with unhappy Spain. Working people, for the most part, in Battersea had organised a bazaar with the object of providing an ambulance for the Spanish Government forces. Strenuous efforts were put forth and much work was voluntarily done. The result, as seen on Tuesday afternoon, was both bright and beautiful. Bazaar stalls were glistening with silver foil and were well laden with goods of the useful sort, plus things to eat. For the most part the lady stallholders were in Spanish costume, which became them admirably, and which we are sure some of them would like to wear on all festal occasions. The broad-brimmed glazed hats looked much more attractive than the shapeless things that so many English ladies balance on the side of their head. The fringed shawls were most graceful. "Borrowed plumes," one of the ladies very regretfully said in our hearing. The bazaar was supplemented by a fun fair and cabaret. It was opened by Mrs. S. Saklatvala, widow of the former Communist M.P. for North Battersea.

OPENING CEREMONY.

woman of Battersea). She was supported by Mrs. Okines, Mrs. Shepherd, members of the North Battersea Co-operative Guild, the organising committee, and the stallholders.

Mrs. Bowler said they had come there with the determination that the bazaar and cabaret should be a success, and that the Battersea ambulance would soon be in Madrid. Every pound spent would send the ambulance another mile further on. The bazaar had taken only about six weeks to organise and arrange, and they would all agree with her that it was a very wonderful effort. The women of Battersea were determined from the start that it was going to be a success. They were determined that their ambulance should go to Spain, and the sooner it went the better they would be pleased. Most of the articles on the stalls were hand-made.

MRS. SAKLATVALA WELCOMED.

Mrs. Saklatvala, who was greeted with loud applause, said she was delighted to be in Battersea once more, where so much of her late husband's work was done. She regarded the invitation to open that bazaar as a tribute to him. There must be many people there who knew that he always insisted on universal brotherhood. He would have appreciated their effort to make common cause for the saving of the lives of the Spanish people. He would have protested against the cold-blooded murder of the civilian adherents of the Spanish Government, and would have warmly supported the provision of an ambulance to save the lives and relieve the suffering of their comrades in Spain.

A vote of thanks to Mrs. Saklatvala was moved by Mrs. Okines, who said she, like many more in Battersea, knew the

The motion was seconded by Mrs. Shepherd and carried with applause.

STALLS AND STALLHOLDERS.

Drapery and Haberdashery (North Battersea Co-operative Guild).—Mrs. Bolton, Mrs. Branson, and Mrs. Grant.

Books.—Mr. W. D. Pritchard.

Fancy Goods and Toys.—Mrs. Wyes, Mrs. Okines, and Miss Murrell.

Woollen and Spanish Goods.—Mrs. Synes, Mrs. May Francis, Mrs. Maisie Storkey, Mrs. Walters, Mrs. Chandler, and Mrs. Stevens.

Groceries.—Mrs. Slack, Mrs. Baker, and Mrs. Pilbey.

White Elephant Stall.—Mrs. Fulsham, Mrs. Brown, Mrs. Robb, Mrs. Evans, and Mrs. Clark.

Hardware.—Mrs. Chantrey and Mrs. Neal.

Carnival Stall.—Mrs. Lewis.

Mystic Stall (character reading).—Mrs. Parsons, Mrs. Speak, Mrs. Ling, and Mrs. Keith.

"Bunty Pulls the Strings."—Mrs. Rumpstead (president of North Battersea Women's Co-operative Guild) and Miss Banks.

Lucky Dip.—Mrs. Findlay.

Bagatelle.—Mr. Miles.

"Spell-it."—Mr. Haynes.

Lucky Arch.—Mr. Smith.

"Spot-'em."—Mr. Whitehead.

Come and Guess.—Mr. Clark.

From 5 to 6 p.m. there was dancing by children, and from 6 to 7 p.m. there was a children's ballet by members of the Battersea Circle, under the direction of Mrs. Vera Cole. At 8 p.m. selections were played by Hayward's Dance Band, and at 8.30 p.m. a Spanish cabaret was given by the Battersea Co-operative players At 9 p.m. Nash's Banjoists took the

Mrs. Saklatvala Opening the Bazaar. The ladies seated are members of the Spanish Aid Committee. Mrs. Bowler, the chairwoman, is the central front figure.

Brigade Dependent's Aid, and the third part to be used for the maintenance of the Battersea ambulance, and any medical supplies that the ambulance may need. Skinners's suggestions were accepted by the Trades Council at its monthly meeting in September.[28]

Although it had achieved the ambulance target, the Trades Council, towards the end of 1938, organised a number of activities on behalf of Spain. This was despite the increasingly bleak prospects for the Republic which was being continually harried by Franco's forces. It was to be a hallmark of the sub-committee that its members remained optimistic throughout, even when the survival of Spanish democracy looked grave.

In September 1938, the Trades Council held a free film show at the Town Hall, at which the pro republican film, 'Spanish Earth' was shown. In November there was a 6d dance at the Town hall which showed a profit of £6. In January 1939, only two months before Franco's triumph, and by which time the Republic had been split in two, the Trades Council organised a children's party. This was in appreciation of Battersea children who had been collecting money for the children of Spain. In a symbolic gesture, six Battersea children were dressed in Spanish costume and were provided with a meal. There was a programme of entertainment, and two films were shown. Each child was given a present of toys, and both the Mayor and Mayoress were in attendance.[29] At Christmas there was the customary carol singing on behalf of Spanish aid. Throughout the conflict the Trades Council organised regular dances at the Town Hall and in addition there were also whist drives and raffles, all of which involved people who might not otherwise have given money to the Republican cause.

During the last six months of the Republic the Trades Council's efforts on behalf of the democratic forces were as great as ever. In December 1938, a letter was sent to Battersea shop keepers asking them to donate food, or money to Spain.[30] In the same month collections were held outside the Granada cinema in Clapham Junction where the film, 'Blockade' was showing. The following month the Aid to Spain committee organised a food week which was very successful. Over 5cwts of food was collected and £20 was given in donations.

The Trades Council also continued with its political pressure on the Government. The demand, even at this late stage, January 1939, was for Spain's right to buy arms. A petition to that effect was taken to 10, Downing Street by the Mayor of Battersea. It was signed by over 2,000 Battersea people, including a majority of local councillors and Battersea North's MP Stephen Sanders.[31]

Throughout the period there were collections at workplaces, and in

Battersea streets, which supplemented the funds raised by social activities. Some of these collections were organised by the Aid to Spain committee, others were organised by ward Labour Party's, or even by sympathetic individuals. There were regular Sunday morning collections. These collections were attacked by the local paper, the 'South Western Star'. In an editorial, the paper claimed that the aid being sent to republican Spain only helped to continue the civil war. The 'South Western Star', told its readers, "these impulsive actions have perhaps only served to prolong the suicidal struggle in Spain".[32] The response to this unwarranted attack on Battersea's aid to Spain activity was swift. Wye, the treasurer of Battersea Labour Party and Trades Council, issued a statement which was published in the paper the following week. Wye claimed that over £1000 had been collected in Battersea since the Spanish war began. This money he said, "had been used for saving lives not destroying them". He outlined the contribution of the Battersea ambulance, which had seen two years service in Spain. He also pointed out that the money collected had been used for Medical Aid, and the Dependents fund for the families of the International Brigaders who had been killed. It was also used to help the Basque children, all of these Wye explained, were 'humanitarian objects' which didn't prolong war. While keen to emphasise this aspect of the aid to Spain movement, Wye also made the political point that Spain should have the right to buy arms. He outlined the work of the Trades Council in this respect, and referred to the petition, which called for Spain's right to purchase arms for its own defence. This petition, he pointed out, had been signed by over 2000 Battersea people, and had been presented to the Prime Minister.[33]

In the month that the Republic fell, March 1939, the Aid to Spain committee reported that it had collected £25, no mean sum in today's terms. The bulk of this, £21, was collected in the Broomwood ward, in the South of the borough, not a particularly promising area for the labour movement. Two months after Franco's victory in Spain, collections were still taking place. A collection in Broomwood ward on June 11th 1939, raised over £10.

Although the Aid to Spain committee had agreed that the money be divided equally, between the Dependents Aid Fund, the Basque Children's fund, and Medical Aid, this did not happen. The last full financial report of the sub-committee was given to the July meeting of the Trades Council, in 1939. Wye reported that £162.8s had gone to the Dependents Aid Fund, £77.10s to Medical Aid, and £75. to the Basque Children's Fund. In addition the committee had donated £64.18.10d to a Spanish aid food ship.[34]

Much of the Aid to Spain committee's work was concerned with humanitarian aid. There was only a very limited political side to the Trades Council's efforts on behalf of Spain. There was the yearly May Day demonstration, when the slogan of Arms for Spain was raised. But there were few Trades Council inspired rallies, or public meetings with Spain as the main theme. There were no Town's Meetings called about Spain. Town's Meeting were a tradition in the borough and could be called by a number (20) of concerned Battersea citizens, who wished to debate or vote on an issue of the day. In the past such meetings had been used to express opposition to unemployment, against intervention in Russia, against the occupation of the Ruhr, and even to protest against the unfair treatment of Battersea citizens by the press. These meetings could attract as many as 1400 people. It is surprising that in the almost three years of the war there was no Town's Meeting called about Spain.

In September 1938, the British battalion of the International Brigade fought its last battle at the River Ebro. In a last desperate effort to save the Republic it was agreed that the soldiers of the International Brigade should be withdrawn. It was hoped that this would put pressure on Germany and Italy to withdraw their troops as well. The move did not succeed. The two fascist powers continued with their war on Spain and the areas held by Franco's rebel forces continued to grow. In January 1939, Barcelona, in the North Eastern end of the now dismembered republic, fell to Franco. Two months later the infant Spanish democracy was finally crushed when Madrid, the capital, was taken, and Franco's forces were triumphant. Even after the fall of the republic the Aid to Spain committee continued to operate. Collections were made for Spanish refugees and there were jumble sales, and door to door collections. It was not until October 1939, over six months after the republic's defeat, that it was finally decided to dissolve the Aid to Spain committee. It was only done then because of the outbreak of war. In the sub-committee's view, hostilities with Germany made it unlikely that aid from Battersea to Spain could ever reach its destination. The recommendation from the sub-committee that it wind up its operations was ratified at a full Trades Council meeting on October 4th, 1939.[35]

In its almost three years existence the Trades Council's Aid to Spain committee had collected £1173.4.10d – almost £50,000 in today's money. It had financed an ambulance, and had made regular donations to the Dependents Aid fund, Medical Aid, and the Basque Children's Fund. In addition it had supplied food and money to the food ships that were sent from Britain to help Spain. In the process thousands of Battersea people by their pennies and their shillings had registered their sympathy for Spain's plight, and their abhorrence of fascism.

The Peace Council

Whilst the spearhead of the aid to Spain movement in Battersea was undoubtedly the Trades Council, the Battersea Peace Council also helped increase awareness about the more general dangers of fascism and war. During the two years of its existence the Council was involved in a number of campaigns to safeguard peace. Whilst not an active participate in gathering support for Republican Spain, the efforts of the Peace Council are worth recording because they did contribute towards an understanding amongst Battersea people of the global consequences of fascist aggression.

The Peace Council was established by the Battersea Labour Party and Trades Council at a conference convened by them at the lower Town Hall in September 1936. There were 86 delegates in attendance representing 6,000 people. Organisations represented included, Trades Unions, ward Labour Party's, Church groups, the Communist Party and the Young Communist League. A provisional committee was elected, and the first secretary was a Mrs H. Parsons (1, Harbut Road). The aim of the Council was to highlight the increasing danger of war.[36]

There was some early friction in the council, and at the first Annual General Meeting, in January 1937, delegates from the Social Credit Party (the Greenshirts) withdrew, because, they claimed, the Peace Council was not fighting against the menace of the banks. Apart from this loss of support the Council was firmly established, and by the time of the AGM some 39 Battersea organisations were affiliated to it.

Throughout 1937 the Council continued to grow. At the monthly meeting in March, the Secretary reported that the number of affiliated organisations had increased to over 50. At the same meeting it was agreed that the council should organise a Battersea Peace Week. However, it was not until two months later, in May 1937, well into the Spanish War, that the Peace Council finally condemned Italian and German aggression in Spain, and urged the Government to raise the matter with the League of Nations. The call was repeated in September with the Peace Council condemning the use of all foreign troops in Spain.

The first Battersea Peace Week took place in October 1937. The week consisted of a whole series of events which focused attention on the threat of war. The first one was organised in conjunction with the Battersea branch of the League of Nations Union. The following year, 1938, the Council sought the assistance of the Trades Council for the week's activities. The Peace Council concerned itself with war, from whatever quarter it came. At the

PEACE MARCHERS TOUR BATTERSEA

Chinese Flag Heads Procession

A new Chinese flag, lent by the Chinese Embassy, was carried at the procession of Battersea Peace Council delegates, who marched through Battersea on Saturday afternoon to protest against Japan's war with China. The Communists' League supplied the music. A start was made from Battersea Town Hall about 3.15 p.m. The marchers carried posters and placards which advocated a boycott of Japanese goods. The route was by Falcon-road, Battersea Park-road, Queen's-road, and Lavender Hill again. Afterwards an open air meeting was held at Comyn-road.

South Western Star, 11th February 1938. "*Boycott Japan*" *Procession at Lavender Hill.*

AGM in January 1938, it was decided to organise a poster parade condemning Japan's invasion of China. The Council advocated the boycotting of Japanese goods, and the demonstrators, carrying banners to that effect, marched along Lavender Hill, Falcon Road and Battersea Park Road. At the Council's next meeting, the demonstration came in for some criticism from Charlie Jones, a delegate from the Battersea Communist Party, and the acting secretary of the Council. He deplored the lack of support for the poster parade, and claimed that, "the YCL came to our rescue. They provided 20 marchers and a band, without which the poster parade would have been a flop."[37] Jones wasn't trying to make a political point. In line with the Communist Party's united front strategy he told the delegates that he didn't want the Peace Council to be dominated by one organisation.

What little dissension and discord there was in the Council was as a result of its being a mixture of pacifist, socialist, trade union, church, and communist organisations. By and large the left, certainly by the middle of 1937, favoured the right of republican Spain to buy arms to defend itself. This was anathema to many christians and pacifists. The Reverend A.G. Prichard, a peace and Labour Party activist in the Borough, resigned from the Labour Party in July 1937, because of his opposition to rearmament.

It was because of this pacifist influence, and the need to keep a united peace front, that the Peace Council was not particularly active on the issue of Spain. There were collections and donations, but they were not on the scale of that organised by the Trades Council. It was not until April 1938, at a meeting with over twenty organisations represented, that the Peace Council finally agreed to support Spain's right to buy arms. This was almost two years into the Spanish war and nearly a year since the Council had first denounced Italian and German aggression in Spain. Even then the there was a move at the meeting to delete that section of the resolution which urged industrial action to bring pressure on the Government to change its policy.[38] The amendment was defeated, which showed not only the strength of the left, but also the by now widespread support that there was for Spanish democracy. This sympathy was affecting the attitudes of even the most ardent of Battersea pacifists.

An indication of this belated concern for Spain was the Peace Council's concluding public meeting for the 1938 Peace Week. On the platform at the Town Hall were Harry Pollitt, the General Secretary of the Communist Party and Langdon Davis, the News Chronicle's correspondent in Spain. The collection was divided evenly between the Dependents Aid Fund and the Battersea Ambulance. This was the first and last public meeting organised by the Peace Council on behalf of Spain. As war approached the activities of the

Peace Council declined. At the July meeting in 1938, the secretary resigned and there were only nine delegates in attendance.[39]

How did Battersea's Aid to Spain movement compare with that of neighbouring areas?

Because of Battersea's record of militancy over the years it is an area that has received a great deal of attention from labour historians. Working class movements in other areas of South London have not been so closely studied. That Battersea did have an effective campaign on behalf of Spain can't be questioned. Because of the Borough's radical and internationalist tradition it was to be expected that its inhabitants would respond in the way that they did. But was Battersea's labour movement any more receptive to Spain's appeal than other areas of South West London? It would be neglectful of the author of this pamphlet if he did not make clear that there was support for Republican Spain in the neighbouring borough of Wandsworth. It is not the purpose of this study to look in detail at that support, but to show that Battersea was not alone in its response to Spain. Someone should chronicle Wandsworth's efforts in this field, so that we can begin to make an assessment of the respective strengths and weaknesses of the Aid to Spain movement in different parts of London.

In Battersea £1100 was collected for Spain. Over £50,000 would be today's equivalent. Nothing like that amount was collected in Wandsworth, but there was regular aid to Spain activity. Wandsworth even had its equivalent to the Battersea ambulance. There were moves to equip and send an ambulance to Bilbao at the cost of £500.

Like Battersea, in Wandsworth much of the aid to Spain activity was conducted by the Trades Council and Borough Labour Party. The first public event was a meeting in the Town Hall organised by the Trades Council, and addressed by the veteran labour movement campaigner, Ben Tillett. This took place in February 1937, some months after the Battersea initiative. The aim of the meeting though was similar, to raise £500 for an ambulance – this was £250 less than the more ambitious Battersea project. Some months later there was another meeting at the Town Hall called by Wandsworth Aid to Spain. The meeting was not a big success, and there was only a small audience. This was despite the showing of the film, 'News from Spain'. Moving pictures could usually attract those who might otherwise not attend a meeting. Mrs Leah Manning spoke and there was a collection of £12 towards the Bilbao ambulance.[40]

What did happen in Wandsworth, unlike Battersea, was that a number of refugee Spanish children from Bilbao were given temporary accommodation. In two unoccupied houses, at 170 and 172, West Hill, 20 children were accommodated for three months. This was arranged by the Putney and Barnes Spanish Relief Committee, which was run entirely by local voluntary support, and included the Rotary Club. What was also surprising was that the local Catholic Ladies Guild gave assistance to the children. In most cases the Catholic Church was more sympathetic to Franco than the Republic.[41]

In another of Battersea's neighbouring areas, Brixton, there were also housed a number of Basque children. F.C.R. Douglas, who was a member of the London County Council and later a Battersea MP, made an appeal for funds for the children through the local press. The Basque children had been living in Brixton since June 1937.[42] By March 1938 the number of Basque children being supported in Brixton had risen to 160.

There was activity in Wandsworth on behalf of the Spanish Republic throughout the three years of the conflict. Even towards the end, when the survival of Spain's fledgling democracy looked slim, this support continued. In the last month before the triumph of Franco, Wandsworth Aid to Spain and the Wandsworth Borough Labour Party and Trades Council held a meeting in the Town Hall. It was called because of 'the serious situation in Spain'. There was a collection of £16, which included £5 from Wandsworth busmen. One of the speakers was John Longstaff, of the Wandsworth Labour League of Youth. He had fought in Spain and had been wounded at the Ebro. In his speech he made a plea for Spain's right to buy arms. Even at this late stage there were many who still believed that the Spanish Republic could win, if it was allowed to compete on equal terms with the fascists.[43] Longstaff had been in the same company as David Guest, the Headquarters Section, and they had known each other from their earlier local activity.[44]

The following week there was another important Aid to Spain meeting in Wandsworth, again at the Town Hall. The meeting, according to local reports, was well attended and the intention was to organise a food collection for Spain. Ted Willis spoke, and so too did G.R. Strauss, the Labour MP for Vauxhall. Once again the demand was for 'Arms for Spain'. In addition there was a call for the British Government not to recognise Franco. Franco's supporters in Britain were asking for his Government to be recognised as the legitimate ruler of Spain.

Some three weeks before Franco's eventual victory, Wandsworth Communists issued a statement saying that it was not yet too late to save Spain. Despite the fall of Barcelona, the Wandsworth Party Local maintained that it was still possible for the democratic forces to win. There were, the communists claimed, "eight million people in Central Spain ready to resist Franco". There must be no recognition of Franco, and financial assistance to the rebels must stop. The statement concluded that, "it is not too late to save Spain, Britain and Peace".[45]

This has been but a glimpse of the Aid to Spain activity in Wandsworth. Its aim has been to show that Battersea was not alone in South West London in its response to the Spanish Republic.

Unity and Disunity

Although there was a united effort on behalf of Spain by Battersea's labour movement, the old animosities between left and right still remained. On the one side were the communists and their supporters, who thought that the labour movement should be united, and that there should be no bans or proscriptions operating against Communist Party members. On the other side were those who had fought against communist influence in the labour movement. They supported the expulsion of communists from the Labour Party, and wanted the ban on communists holding positions in the Trades Unions and Trades Councils to continue. These two groups had fought a running battle within the local labour movement for over ten years. Although the anti communists had to all intents and purpose triumphed by 1928, there was still a good deal of sympathy for the communists from amongst some activists in the Battersea Labour Party and Trades council. Many who did not agree with the communists were still opposed to their expulsion from the Labour Party. In addition a number of communists were prominent in the local trade union movement, and commanded respect. Although they were denied official positions, this did not prevent them from exerting an influence within the ranks of the Labour and Trades Council. These long running disagreements resurfaced during the Spain campaign, and although they were largely overcome they were an indication of the deep division that still affected, not only the local labour movement, but the national movement as well.

It was the Battersea communists who had initiated the Aid to Spain movement in the Borough, and had organised the first meetings. In addition it was Communist Party members on the Labour Party and Trades Council who had first suggested that an Aid to Spain committee be established. When this committee was formed, in December 1936, the first secretary was a communist, Tom Oldershaw, who was later killed in Spain.

The old antagonism towards the communists first became apparent at the Trades Council meeting in May 1937. The first item on the agenda was the eligibility of delegates under the TUC rules. In 1935 the TUC, at its annual Congress had narrowly passed a motion that no member of the Communist Party could be a delegate to a Trades Council. Many Trades Unions and Trades Council's simply ignored this ruling and refused to carry it out. After a discussion, delegates to the Battersea Trades Council agreed that two delegates, who were both Communist Party members, should be asked to leave. These were Jack Lye from the Shop Assistants Union and Dan Lewis from the Transport and General Workers Union. Both left the meeting. In addition Tom Oldershaw gave up the secretaryship of the Aid to Spain Committee because, "he was no longer eligible". He was thanked on behalf on the Trades Council for his work.[46] This action did not go unchallenged. A local branch of the Amalgamated Engineering Union sent in a resolution protesting at the expulsion of what they called, 'left wing delegates'. The Secretary of the Trades Council in his reply to the branch, said that only Communist Party members, and not left wing delegates, had been expelled. There was also a protest from the Battersea branch of the National Union of Clerks. In a resolution, the branch deplored the removal of Communist Party members, and supported united action between the Battersea Communist Party and Labour Party in the Spain campaign. In both cases the actions taken by the Trades Council were endorsed by the delegates.

The hostility towards the Battersea communists was expressed at the highest level. G. Fineran, the Secretary of the Battersea Labour Party and Trades Council, was a delegate to the 1937 Annual Labour Party Conference. Fineran was a long time opponent of the communists, and had been instrumental in establishing an official Labour and Trades Council in Battersea in July 1926, after the disaffiliation of the old Trades Council for refusing to expel communists. Fineran told the Conference delegates that they must retain control of the aid to Spain movement. Speaking to a resolution which sought to reverse the previous year's decision when the Party had supported non-intervention, Fineran urged the delegates to follow Battersea's example. He told them that in Battersea the campaign for Spain was completely controlled by the local Labour Party and Trades Council,

> I just want to give a little advice here to the people who are to conduct this campaign in the constituencies to follow the example we in Battersea are carrying out. We have sent an ambulance out to Spain. The Battersea Labour Party and Trades Council carries out and controls the whole of the organisation in Battersea, and we are not associated with anyone; there is no other body associated with us. We are the people who control and direct it, and unless you do the same, the other people will cash in on your efforts, and get away with them, just as the previous speaker has paid tribute to the Communist Party. It is about time a tribute was paid to our own Party for the work they have been doing in the constituencies.

> I am the responsible Secretary of the Battersea Trades Council and Labour Party, and I say that unless the Constituency Parties in this nation-wide campaign are very careful and watch and take a very strong and direct control, then the other people will cash in on it, not only the Communist Party, but other people who want to gain kudos out of it. The National party and the Executive can issue instructions for the campaign to be carried out, but it is we in the constituencies who have to carry it out, and we have got to see to it in its carrying out that no-one else controls it but ourselves.[47]

Fineran's remarks naturally caused some resentment amongst Battersea communists. It was they who had been instrumental in starting the aid to Spain campaign locally, at a time when the Labour Party nationally still supported non-intervention. The communists were now working like trojans for a united effort against fascism, and expressed concern at Fineran's splitting tactics.[48]

Apart from these one or two upsets the united front against fascism worked well in Battersea. The Aid to Spain movement did hold together, and some of the excesses of both sides in the 'Class against Class' period of 1928-1934 were beginning to be forgotten. (It was during this earlier period that the communists had castigated Labour Party members as Social Fascists).

Although local united action over Spain was achieved, it did not prevent both parties from organising separate events, demonstrations and marches. Often the two went hand in hand. At a Town's Meeting towards the end of 1936, Dan Lewis from the Communist Party accused the fascists of being warmongers, and urged help for Spain. He was supported by Barratt from the Battersea Socialist League, and the meeting declared in favour of co-operation for peace. Yet the following May Day both the Battersea Communist Party and the Battersea Labour Party and Trades Council organised separate demonstrations. The Labour Party mobilised over 2000 people who marched on the Sunday from the Town Hall. The Communist Party organised their demonstration the day before, on the Saturday. They too met at the Town Hall and the procession went via North Street in Clapham to Hyde Park. The Communist Party demonstration had Spain very much to the fore. On the communists' banner were inscribed the names of six Battersea men who had gone to Spain. These were, Eddie Bee, Bert Sines, Ralph Fox, David Halloran, Martin Messer, and Mike Kelly.[49]

Although the two organisations held separate 1937 May Day demonstrations, a few months later the Battersea Communist Party called for full support for a Labour Party demonstration on behalf of Spain in Trafalgar Square. The communists placed an advertisement in the local paper, and 130 of them and their supporters marched from Battersea via Nine Elms to Trafalgar Square.

A further indication of the growing unity against fascism was an event at

SUPPORT
LABOUR RALLY
TRAFALGAR SQUARE
THIS SUNDAY, JULY 11, 3.30 p.m.

BATTERSEA!

Battersea has sent Bert Sines, Ralph Fox, David Halloran, Martin Messer, Mike Kelley, Comrade Baker, Eddie Bee, and George Leeson to fight in the International Brigade

TO DEFEND DEMOCRACY AGAINST FASCISM

The "Daily Herald" reports Contingents from all over London are to march on Trafalgar Square.

BATTERSEA MUST MARCH TOO
YOU are Battersea

MEET at "PRINCE'S HEAD" 1.45 p.m.
Leave at 2 p.m.

MARCH IN SUPPORT OF LABOUR!
ARMS FOR THE SPANISH GOVERNMENT!

South Western Star, 9th July, 1937.

the Town Hall later in the year to celebrate the twentieth anniversary of the Russian revolution. This was organised by the local branch of the Friends of the Soviet Union. Paul Robeson was the star attraction. He both sang and spoke, and according to local reports the pavements outside the Town Hall were crowded for hours beforehand. Reg Bishop of the Communist Party, and Saklatvala's old secretary, chaired the meeting, and the main speaker was the Labour MP George Strauss.[50]

The united front against fascism continued to make progress in the borough, and by 1938 Battersea communists and Labour Party members were as often as not involved in joint activity against the common enemy. The May Day march that year was a united effort, and headed off from the Town Hall with the South West London YCL Bugle band leading the way. In the following September there was a memorial meeting for Tom Oldershaw and David Guest, both International Brigaders, and Communist Party members, who had been killed in Spain. The meeting was jointly organised by the Labour Party and Trades Council, the Battersea Communist Party and the Young Communist League. There was a memorial march from Queens Circus, and a slow march via Battersea Park Road, Lavender Hill and Falcon Road. Both the large and small halls at the Town Hall were booked for the occasion. Inside there were large portraits of the other men associated with Battersea who had died in Spain, Ralph Fox, Martin Messer, Mick Kelly and David Halloran. On the platform in the hall there were two empty chairs decked with laurel leaves and a huge banner proclaimed, "They will live forever in the memory of the Battersea workers". The speakers reflected all sections of the labour movement and included Ivor Montague and Ted Bramley from the Communist Party, local Labour Party and Trades Council speakers and the leaders of both the dead men's trade unions, the Amalgamated Society of Woodworkers and the Shop Assistants Union.[51]

By now it was generally recognised by both sides in the Battersea labour movement that the fascists did not distinguish between marxist and non marxist socialists, all were the enemy and had to be eradicated. It was a view that had been expressed some eighteen months before, soon after the Spanish war started. R. Freeman, the Labour parliamentary candidate for Portsmouth had addressed an Aid to Spain meeting in Battersea. He had told his audience, "what consolation was it to a Labourist or a Communist to differ on party policy when both were suffering under the whip of a fascist bully in a concentration camp".[52] They were words that were now beginning to ring true.

Fascism and Anti-Fascism

Although between the years 1936–39, the Battersea labour movement was preoccupied with helping Republican Spain, that did not prevent the activists in the borough from conducting an all out onslaught on fascism. There was consistent guerrilla warfare against any attempt by Franco's supporters in Britain to gain a foothold in the area. Paramount amongst these supporters were Mosley's British Union of Fascists – the blackshirts.

On a number of occasions Mosley attempted to speak in the borough, usually to be confronted by a hostile and well organised anti-fascist crowd. But the fascists had their successes. There was an organised fascist presence in Battersea and it kept up a stream of intermittent activity throughout the Spanish war. It would be wrong to think that because of the tremendous response that Spain elicited amongst the Battersea labour movement that there was no opposition – there was, but the fascists in the area were isolated from the

---

ANTI-FASCIST
PUBLIC MEETING
BATTERSEA TOWN HALL
(LOWER HALL)

SUNDAY, MAY 29, 1938
Doors Open 7.30 p.m.

Speakers:
Mrs. C. S. GANLEY, J.P., L.C.C.
Prof. HALDANE,
Mr. LANGDON DAVIES,
and Mr. HAROLD SMITH.
Chairman: COUNCILLOR W. WYE

South Western Star, 27th May 1938.

36

organised working class and never gained a following like they did in the east end of London.

Battersea's response to fascism was sharp. Soon after the accession of Hitler to power in March 1933, there was a meeting in the borough called by the newly established Relief Committee for the Victims of German Fascism. After some initial controversy it was decided that Saklatvala should be asked to address the meeting which took place at the Town Hall in July 1933. Other speakers at the meeting were James Maxton from the Independent Labour Party, Professor Haldane, and Hannen Swaffer from the 'Daily Herald'.[53]

The coming to power of the Nazis also affected Battersea's Jewish community. They responded to the plight of the Jewish refugees, whose numbers increased once Hitler's anti-Semitic laws were in place. Battersea and Wandsworth Jews formed a self denial group at the South West London Synagogue on Bolingbroke Grove. Members of the group agreed to pay a certain amount each week for the upkeep of Jewish children from Germany. This was later extended to include all refugee children from Nazism.

While many in Battersea were aghast at the rise of fascism in Italy and Germany, there were some in the Borough who were sympathetic. The British Union of Fascists saw Battersea as a possible recruitment ground, and established their Unemployed Section's Headquarters there, on Lavender Hill. In July 1933, the Battersea Communist Party, as part of their campaign against Hitler, organised an anti-fascist open air meeting, very close to the fascist premises. There was an audience of about five hundred and BUF supporters tried to heckle the speakers. The meeting was advertised as, "the first in a series aimed at building the united front against fascism in North Battersea."[54]

In order to establish some credibility the fascists took on some local issues, traditionally the sort of thing done by the left. They mounted an all night guard to prevent the eviction of a tenant in Orkney Street in North Battersea. They even arranged transportation for the tenant's furniture to a neighbouring house. For their efforts the fascists received some publicity in the press.[55]

A portent of what was to come occurred the following year, in February 1934. A crowd of 1200 gathered in the Battersea Town Hall to listen to speeches by prominent Communist Party leaders, including Wal Hannington of the Unemployed Workers Movement. During the singing of the 'International' a disturbance was started by a group of 30 fascists. The communist 'Daily Worker' warned, "it is essential that at all future meetings of this kind proper precautions should be taken to see that people of this type are not allowed to break up working class meetings."[56] It was an indication, if any were needed, that although Battersea had a fine record of internationalism and socialism there were still those in the borough who took a different view.

In October 1936, soon after the outbreak of the Spanish war, and at the same time as the famous Battle of Cable Street, Battersea's fascists were banned from holding a meeting in the Town Hall. In response they announced that they were to hold a public open air meeting the following week in Comyn Road, near Clapham Junction. John Beckett, a prominent figure in the BUF, and a former Labour MP, was billed to speak. When the fascists arrived to begin their meeting they discovered that the communists had got there first and had taken over their spot. They were forced to move one street along, to Aliwal Street. Beckett was booed by a crowd of about 500. The fascists managed to give out some leaflets, which claimed that the Labour controlled Borough Council had 'given in to Red terror'. In retaliation for this setback, a few days later the local blackshirts attempted to disrupt an anti-fascist meeting in the Town Hall. At this meeting Clive Branson from the Communist Party, and Councillor Lewin from the Labour Party, were the main speakers. Here too the fascists were thwarted, this time by an array of anti-fascist stewards. As a last resort, unable to get into the meeting, the blackshirts shouted out, 'down with the Yids', outside the Town Hall.[57]

The successful stopping at Cable Street, in October 1936, of Mosley's proposed march through the east end of London, had a demoralising effect on London's fascists. After this, Blackshirt activity in Battersea was at a low ebb. This did not prevent some of Battersea's more militant workers from being acutely aware of the ever present dangers of fascism. Amongst the Battersea busmen, who made regular collections for Spain, there was a strong anti-fascist feeling. During the unofficial busmen's strike in May 1937, the Battersea Busmen's banner had written on it the inscription, "Workers smash fascism and war".

There was little reported fascist activity in the area until March 1938. Then the blackshirts decided to renew their efforts to gain a toehold in the borough. Mosley applied for the use of the Town Hall for a meeting. His application was discussed by the Trades and Labour Council. The Trades Council delegates were not all of a like mind. While some opposed letting Mosley have the Town Hall, others were in favour. In the end the Trades Council recommended that the matter be referred to the Labour Group on the Borough Council for their consideration. Battersea's Labour majority declined the blackshirts' request, on the grounds that they could not allow disorderly meetings to take place in council property.

In the same week that the BUF's application for a meeting place was

38

turned down, the Battersea Labour Party and Trades Council organised their own meeting, to protest against Hitler's annexation of Austria. Stephen Sanders, the local MP, and Caroline Ganley, were the main speakers. There was also a demonstration against the annexation in Trafalgar Square, at which a contingent from the Battersea Labour League of Youth were present. They afterwards demonstrated outside the German Embassy.[58]

Denied the use of the Town Hall, the Battersea branch of the BUF organised a march from Clapham Junction to Clapham Common in the last week of March. There were 80-100 marchers present, and they were preceded by a fife and drum band. The branch also had its own banner, which was carried on the demonstration. At the Common a crowd of 300-400 people turned up for the meeting, and there was constant heckling. One of the principal fascist demands was, 'the sending of Jews to Palestine, without return tickets'. After the meeting there was another march, this time to Queens Circus where the fascists held another rally.[59]

This local BUF initiative was a foretaste of what was to come. Mosley, unable for a second time to hold a meeting at the Town Hall, announced that he would speak instead at an open air meeting in Battersea at Comyn Road, on Monday, April 4th. The Battersea fascists advertised their leader's intention, by chalking the time and date of the meeting on the streets. (Chalking, before the war, was a common way of advertising a meeting or demonstration). Anti-fascists responded to Mosley's declaration, and there was a call for a counter demonstration. The Battersea Communist Party, on the day before Mosley was due to make his arrival, organised a mass leafleting session from the People's Bookshop. In addition, the 'Daily Worker' urged its readers to demonstrate against Mosley.

On the day Mosley did speak but the event was violent. The fascists placed a platform in Comyn Road a few days beforehand, which they guarded day and night. Mosley did not use this platform but spoke from a covered van instead. He addressed the crowd with two microphones and six loudspeakers. He was jeered and heckled throughout with shouts of 'Arms for Spain' and 'Down with fascism.' Police were called in from Camberwell and Wandsworth. A plate glass window in Hawes drapery shop in Clapham Junction was broken, and so too was a window of the People's Bookshop on Lavender Hill. The local branch of the BUF also had its Head Quarters on Lavender Hill, at Number 263. There were fights throughout the day between fascists and anti-fascists and ten arrests were made.[60]

Although the fascists had received a mauling at Comyn Road, they continued with their efforts in the borough. At a public meeting organised by

South Battersea Labour Party, and addressed by the Labour leader, Clement Attlee, they overturned chairs in order to disrupt the event. Two fascists who shouted, 'Heil Hitler', and 'Heil Mosley' were ejected from the meeting. In the same week activists in the local labour movement organised an anti-fascist public meeting at the Town Hall, at which there was no disruption.

There was not always resistance to fascist activity in Battersea. Three months after the Mosley affair about 150 fascists marched virtually unmolested from Altenburg Gardens on Lavender Hill, to Queens Circus, where they held a rally. The two speakers, William Pogson and Ernest Clark, were listened to by a sympathetic audience, and very little jeering or heckling took place. About 250 marchers then returned to Altenburg Gardens, again with no opposition.

This march was probably the local blackshirts' last gasp. Recognition of what was happening in Germany, and Hitler's designs on expansion, were beginning to make the home grown form of fascism look less attractive. This repugnance of fascism was now felt by all sectors of Battersea society. The intensity and breadth of the aid to Spain movement in the Borough had made a major contribution towards developing this anti-fascist feeling. The thousands of Battersea people who had given money for Spain had at the same time, although not always in a conscious way, registered their abhorrence of fascism, and their support for democracy. The scale of the movement in the Borough ensured that it reached out to large numbers of people who might not otherwise have been touched by gestures of international solidarity. True, there was tradition to draw on, but Aid to Spain mobilised thousands in Battersea, and played a major role in ensuring that fascism was never able to make inroads, either into the local labour movement, or amongst the people of the borough.

Defeat, and other battles

The International Brigades were withdrawn from Spain in October 1938. It was a last desperate attempt by the Republic to halt the unending supply of men and munitions that were pouring into the Franco held areas. The Republican Government hoped by such action to persuade Britain and France to put pressure on Germany and Italy to induce them to abide by the non-intervention policy. It was to no avail. Barcelona fell to Franco in January 1939, and two months later the Republic was defeated. It had been a magnificent but one sided battle. Little Spain had taken on the armed might of the two formidable fascist powers. For almost three years she had waged an uphill fight – with ill trained and poorly equipped troops Spain had shown the world that democracy was worth fighting for. But to Spain's side had rallied the world's democratic forces, and from every part of the globe men and women left their homes and their loved ones in order to defend Spain's right to be free – many made the ultimate sacrifice. The International Brigades gathered together some of the most self-sacrificing and courageous human beings of their generation.

Apart from these fighting forces, Spain's plight also mobilised millions of others to sacrifice what little they had to render the Republic assistance. There were aid to Spain movements in every part of Britain, and in nearly every country of the world. Pennies and pesos, dollars and drachmas, francs and pfennigs, all were sent to help the Spanish people's brave fight. Food ships ran the illegal fascist blockade to ensure that Spain did not starve. English sailors, along with those of many other countries, died in the waters off Spain in a desperate bid to bring in supplies. Internationally only the Soviet Union defied the non-intervention policy and gave Spain assistance. It was therefore with a heavy heart that anti fascists, after three years of endeavours, saw the Republic defeated. In Battersea, as we have seen, aid continued to the Republican refugees, even after Franco's triumph.

By the end of 1938, with the war nearing its depressing climax, the Battersea labour movement lifted its spirits by organising a welcome back meeting for some of the Battersea men and women who had fought in Spain. The Battersea Labour Party and Trades Council organised the meeting, and booked both halls in the Town Hall. The meeting took place on December 11th 1938. On the platform were many of those who had been to Spain. Clive Branson, Bert Sines, Eddie Bee, Joe Ilean, the ambulance driver, and Nurse Jones. The meeting was preceded by a march from Queens Circus to the Town Hall. Inside the Hall there was a roll of honour of those associated with the Battersea labour movement, who had lost their lives in Spain. Also on display was a chart, which showed how much money had been collected by the local aid to Spain committee. At the meeting itself there was a collection of £60. Apart from those on the platform who spoke, there were also speeches from representatives of Battersea Labour Party, and Dan Lewis from the Battersea Communist Party.

As the Spanish war drew to its close the Battersea labour movement began to focus on issues that the war had raised. Chief among these was the threat of aerial bombardment. The Spanish town of Guernica, which had been reduced to rubble by German and Italian planes, and had been made famous by Picasso's painting, highlighted the dangers of war from the air. In Battersea, with its factories, power station and railway network, the perils of bombing in any future war was particularly acute. In September 1938, the local Communist

Party organised a meeting in the Town Hall with the theme of, 'getting a real ARP in Battersea'. The ARP was Air Raid Precaution. Speakers at the meeting also demanded that the peace of Europe should be safeguarded by an alliance of Britain and the Soviet Union, against the fascist powers. It was a demand that was echoed by the Battersea branch of the Labour League of Youth. In the same month they sent a letter to the Government which called for a 'firm line against appeasers', and the, 'territorial integrity of Czechoslovakia'. The League of Youth branch further demanded the formation of a peace bloc between France, Britain, the United States and the USSR. It also wanted, 'solidarity with the victims of aggression in China, Spain, Austria, and Abyssinia'.

It was apparent by early 1939 that a European war was approaching. The Battersea Communist Party continued with its call of Arms for Spain, but now there was a greater urgency. The Party branch denounced the recently signed Munich agreement as, 'a surrender to the fascist powers', and urged the Chamberlain Government to form an alliance with France, the USSR and America, against Germany and Italy.[61] In February 1939, Harry Pollitt spoke at the Town Hall, and not only emphasised the dangers of fascist aggression, but also the need for an adequate defence, in the event of war breaking out. The meeting included a film, 'If war should come', which showed the dangers of aerial bombardment. The Battersea communists also continued with their political offensive against fascism. In March 1939, along with others in the local labour movement, they helped form a group in support of Stafford Cripps, who had been expelled from the Labour Party for advocating a united front of all left parties against fascism. The group met regularly at the Library on Lavender Hill.

In a practical way too the Battersea communists exposed the dangers of war. In the month after the defeat of the Spanish Republic, the local party branch issued a penny pamphlet entitled, 'A Real ARP for Battersea'. It was an extremely comprehensive programme of how the area could be defended against attack from the air. It was detailed, and its recommendations costed, and it gave a blow by blow account of just what would happen to Battersea's population if hostilities broke out and bombing started. It was also prophetic. A year before the blitz took place the pamphlet warned that an enemy (i.e. Germany), "will try to terrorise the population by bombing". It also showed Battersea's vulnerability to aerial attack. There was a power station, a gas works, a major railway station, and 120 factories within the Borough boundary. Two of these factories were producing war material. In addition, the pamphlet pointed out that the area was easy to locate from the air. The Power Station and the river would act as excellent guides for enemy bombers.

The Battersea communists proposed that 33,000 Battersea people be evacuated immediately war broke out. These would include 18,000 children, 10,000 toddlers and babies in arms with their mothers, plus all old people and invalids. Evacuation should be encouraged but not compulsory, as the communists believed that many Battersea women would not want to leave their husbands. The whole process should be organised around evacuation committees at each Battersea school. The committees should consist of teachers and mothers. That would leave 110,000 people still in Battersea. These would need protecting. The pamphlet proposed that deep shelters be dug in South Battersea, and parts of North Battersea where this was possible. It would not be feasible along by the river where the soil was waterlogged. It was also proposed that an underground road be built from the river to Clapham Junction. In addition shelters should be constructed for all those working in factories in the Borough, and also for those people living in the St. Johns Estate on St. Johns Hill.

The money for such a scheme, which would cost £1,210,000, should be a grant of seventy-five per cent from the Government. The rest to be raised by the Borough Council, by a tax on local industry, which at present was let off of three quarters of its rates. In conclusion, the communists made clear their opposition to the Borough Council's proposal to build trenches on Clapham Common at a cost of £7,000. They maintained that the money could be better spent 'on real protection'.[62]

The pamphlet was a grandiose endeavour, and illustrated the concerns of many in the local labour movement over the effects of a coming war. The Battersea communists, like their colleagues in the Labour Party and Trades Council, now that the Spanish war had been concluded, turned their attention to other matters. While Spanish democracy seemed to have a chance of survival, all the activists in the Battersea movement worked might and main to ensure its possible success. Once it was realised that this was not to be, their efforts went into other areas of struggle. Spain's defeat brought war closer, and with Franco's victory the local labour movement redoubled its efforts to win a united front against fascism, as the only guarantee of peace.

This was the theme of Battersea's last May Day demonstration before war broke out. Two thousand five hundred marched from Queens Circus to Hyde Park. The Battersea Labour Party contingent carried banners advertising the plight of the concentration camp victims, while the communists demanded that, 'Chamberlain must go'. The Battersea labour movement was united as never before. All sides saw the danger emanating from Germany, and all wanted a stand to be made against fascism.

The Spanish war had ensured, that in Battersea anyway, the labour movement was aware of fascist aggression. The three years spent collecting for Republican Spain had left its imprint on the local movement. The fight for Spanish democracy, although defeated, had helped unite a previously disunited labour movement. The solidarity of Battersea people with Spain, not only helped sustain the Republic, but in turn it made many in the Borough aware of the dangers of fascism. It was no consolation for those defeated Spanish democrats who suffered at Franco's hands, but the Spanish war did help develop an international understanding of what fascism meant. It ensured that when war finally came the people of Battersea, and Britain, would fight with a tenacity and endeavour that could come only from an understanding of what they were fighting against. How true rang Pollitt's words, uttered on the aftermath of the shameful Munich betrayal, "the appetite of the fascist tiger grows with each fresh kill. Can we be so blind as not to see that our turn will come unless we make a stand now."[63]

There is little doubt that if that stand had been made on behalf of Spanish Democracy in 1936, the Republic would have triumphed and the fascist aggressors would have suffered their first defeat. It would have ensured that the ultimate fight against fascism could have been concluded that much quicker.

The Battersea Volunteers

> We came because our open eyes could see no other way. [C. Day Lewis].

> To live at such a time as this and take part in so magnificent a struggle is the greatest honour that can fall to anybody. ... This is one of the most decisive battles ever fought for the future of the human race, and all personal considerations fade into insignificance by the side of it.

So wrote the Battersea volunteer, David Guest, in a letter to his mother from Spain, a few months before his death. His sentiments, and reasons for fighting, were also expressed by the Spanish Prime Minister Dr. Negrin, in his farewell speech to the International Brigades in Barcelona in October 1938.

> You Internationals came to Spain to defend our country, not on the order of any hierarchy, but of your own free will, to sacrifice, if necessary, that which is the most difficult of all things to sacrifice- life. You came to defend justice and right because you know full well that here in Spain, the liberty of the world was at stake.... Your spirit, and the spirit of your dead, will remain forever a part of history.

The Spanish war inspired men and women from all over the world to leave their own country, in order to fight on behalf of Spanish democracy. Over two thousand went from Britain, and many joined the British battalion of the International Brigade.

The Brigade was formed on the initiative of the Communist International.

Initially the British Battalion was to be called after Battersea's own ex MP, Shapurji Saklatvala. The suggestion of this name for the Battalion was first raised by Ralph Fox, in a letter to Harry Pollitt from Spain. Ralph Fox, who was one of the first to volunteer, was living in the Battersea area at the time of his enlistment. Although it was agreed in England that the Battalion be named after Saklatvala, who had died a few months before the war broke out, this name was never popular in Spain, and there it was always referred to simply as the British battalion.

Six men who were associated with Battersea lost their lives in Spain. At the time of their departure they were active in the Battersea labour movement. The majority did not come from the Borough, but had made the area their home. They were a diverse group. David Guest from Cambridge, and Ralph Fox from Halifax, were two intellectuals, one a scientist, the other a writer. Tom Oldershaw was a carpenter, who lived in Balham. Martin Messer, a young railway clerk, originated from Glasgow. David Halloran was from Middlesbrough, and Mick Kelly from Ireland. All were known, loved, and respected for their sacrifice, by Battersea's working class movement. Something of the depth of this reverence can be seen in the memorial meeting that took place for Tom Oldershaw and David Guest at the Battersea Town Hall. The meeting remembered not just those two, but the four others from Battersea who had made the supreme sacrifice. As Councillor W.J. Wye recalls,

> it (the meeting) was a real manifestation of the deep affection the people of Battersea had for him (David Guest) and Tom Oldershaw. Several thousand men and women, including forty members of the International Brigade marched to the Town Hall to the slow beat of muffled drums of the South West London Youth Band, and the North London Workers Band. Portrait banners of David and Tom were carried by the marchers and a roll of honour bearing the names of Ralph Fox, D. Halloran, Mick Kelly and Martin Messer, other Battersea men killed in Spain. Battersea has seldom, if ever, witnessed so impressive a demonstration. The streets were lined with a tremendous crowd of sympathetic onlookers. The procession was nearly a mile long and it took an hour and a half to reach its destination. Both large and small halls were packed while an overflow meeting was held outside.
>
> On the main platform were representative speakers from all sections of the organised working class movement, while two empty chairs with laurel leaves were placed one each side of the chairman. A hundred pounds was collected for a fund for the dependents of the men of the International Brigade.
>
> The speeches will live for ever in the memory of those present, for both speakers and audience displayed such sincerity and devotion in paying their last respects to these two great comrades.

There was also a huge banner inside the hall with the inscription, "they will live for ever in the memory of the Battersea workers".[64]

Battersea's proud tradition of internationalism and solidarity with the oppressed had expressed itself yet again with the death in Spain of some of its finest labour movement activists. With little but their courage and convictions to protect them these Battersea martyrs had laid down their lives for the sake of freedom. While Germany and Italy had tested their latest weapons on the battlefields of Spain, they, and thousands like them, had rallied to the Republic's defence.

Against all the odds, for almost three years Spain had resisted the fascist embrace. But while Germany and Italy had led the frontal onslaught on Spanish democracy, fascism's backdoor sympathisers in Britain had sabotaged the Republic's efforts to protect itself by pushing through the policy of non-intervention. While the nation's leaders fraternised with Franco, it was left to the labour movement to defend freedom. Apart from those who made the supreme sacrifice, others went from Battersea and helped the Republican forces. Of these many survived, and their experiences in Spain were to prove invaluable in the anti-fascist war, that finally came six months after the Republic's defeat. These volunteers carried the flame of internationalism that had burned brightly amongst Battersea's working class for almost half a century, and ensured that it would not be extinguished by democracy's foes. They, like many in the Borough, knew full well, long before their rulers, that bombs on Madrid meant bombs on London.

The Battersea Volunteers who went to Spain with their place of origin, if known

Below is a list of those who went from Battersea to Spain. There may be others, and information about some is sparse. I have included short biographies about some of the volunteers where information is known. For some of the volunteers there is very little surviving information and the author would be grateful if anyone reading this pamphlet could supply further details.

Ralph Fox, Halifax, killed at Cordoba, December 1936.
David Guest, London, killed at the Ebro, July 1938.
David Halloran, Middlesbrough, killed at Jarama, February 1937.
Michael Kelly, Ballinsaloe, Ireland, killed at Brunete, July 1937.
Martin Messer, Glasgow, killed at Boadilla, December 1936.
Tom Oldershaw, London, killed at Aragon, March 1938.
G.W. Baker
Edwin Bee
J Broomfield
Clive Branson

Percy Cohen
Joe Ilean
George Leeson

Nurse Jones, A. Watts, Wheeler and **Heath,** are also mentioned as having been to Spain. The author can find no record of them in the International Brigade Archive. Further information would be most welcome. References to the above four individuals are as follows:

Nurse Jones was referred to in an advert for the welcome back meeting for the Battersea members of the International Brigade in December 1938. Her name was linked with Clive Branson, Bert Sines and Joe Ilean, all of whom had been to Spain. See 'South Western Star' December 9th, 1938

A. Watts. There is no reference to an A. Watts in the International Brigade Archive. He sent a letter to the Battersea Trades Council in January 1938, describing his experiences on the way to joining the International Brigade. See Battersea Labour Party and Trades Council sub-committee Minutes 30th January, 1938.

Wheeler and **Heath** are referred to in the Battersea Trades and Labour Council sub-committee Minutes for 30th April, 1939. It was stated that they had returned from Spain. The only Wheeler referred to in the International Brigade Archive, is Robert Wheeler who helped the Quakers with their relief work.

There are no references to Heath in the I.B. Archive, apart from Edward Heath, who was a Tory student leader at the time, and who visited Spain. He had no connection with Battersea.

It must be pointed out that the International Brigade Archive, extensive though it is, does not carry information on all the volunteers. Because the four above are not listed, it does not mean that they did not go to Spain.

Short Biographies of the Battersea Volunteers

Edwin (Eddy) Bee

A member of Church Ward Labour Party in Battersea, he was an architect in a London firm before his enlistment. He became the Chief of the Brigade's Topography Department and held the rank of Lieutenant. See 'Book of the 15th Brigade' Published by Commissariat of War, Madrid 1938. See also letter to 'South Western Star' February 5th, 1937.

Clive Branson

Before his enlistment he lived at 4, Glycena Road, off Lavender Hill. In the early days of the war he acted as a courier for recruits to the International

Brigade. For more details see Noreen Branson reminiscences. He went to Spain in January 1938, and was captured without firing a shot. "The disappointment was terrible.... I nearly burst into tears" ('South Western Star' November 18th, 1938). He was imprisoned until released in October 1938, by which time the International Brigade had been withdrawn. He described his experiences in a Franco concentration camp at a Battersea Communist Party meeting in November 1938.

> They worked hard to keep up moral – some men got frightened – prisoners were beaten, there were no cigarettes- some would fight over a butt end. The food was rotten. They organised games and a chess tournament. The chessmen were made out of pieces of soap. They also drew packs of cards on any scraps of paper that they could find. The biggest difficulties were personal bickerings and petty disputes

See 'South Western Star' November 18th, 1938.

Ralph Fox

He was born in Halifax, West Yorkshire, in 1900. In his early twenties he helped the Society of Friends with their famine relief work in the Samara region of Africa. Upon his return he worked in the Propaganda Department of the Communist Party. In 1924, he moved to the 'Sunday Worker'. He left there in 1927 to spend three years at the Marx Engels Institute in the USSR. For a short period he was the Literary Editor of the 'New Statesman'.

He was killed at the battle of Cordoba in December 1936 while making a personal reconnaissance ahead of the most advanced troops. At the time of his enlistment he lived at 17, Lucas House, Larkhall Estate, Wandsworth Road. He was the author of 'The Novel and the People', and many other works.

David Guest

He was the son of a Labour MP, Dr Hayden Guest. He joined the Communist Party at Cambridge in 1931. He was active in the student branch and helped form the town branch of the party. In 1933 he moved to Battersea and established the People's Bookshop at 115, Lavender Hill. He became a member of the Battersea Branch of the Shop Assistants Union and was a delegate from the branch to the Trades Council. An active member of the Battersea branch of the Young Communist League he organised the first Youth Peace Parade in the area. In May 1935, fifty young people, some dressed up as nurses, others in gas masks and with stretchers, helped expose the horror of war. He was also the instigator of a youth swimming club in Battersea. According to Bob Gorham, the former secretary of the Battersea YCL, ' David would go out whitewashing until 2 or 3 in the morning'.

He lived with the Sines family in Bolingbroke Grove. David was in the same company, the Headquarters Section, as Bert Sines.

OPEN LETTER TO THE YOUTH OF ALL COUNTRIES

Dear Comrade,

We Spanish and English-speaking youth of the 15th. International Brigade, who are playing our part in the fight against fascism in Spain, appeal to you in this decisive war in which the future of the world is at stake, to come to our aid.

The entire people, in the rear as well as at the front, is throwing itself enthusiastically into the work of winning the war. More united and determined than ever before, the Spanish people is confident that it can beat off the fascist invaders.

In this struggle we have lost many of the finest of our comrades, the best representatives of the youth of all countries. They have been sacrificed to the murderous fascist war machine because the Government of democratic countries have denied to the Spanish Republic the right to purchase arms for its self-defense.

We ask the youth of the democratic countries this question. How long are you going to permit your Governments to carry through this infamous betrayal of democracy, to be the accomplices of Hitler and Mussolini in this murder? Can you be satisfied that you are doing all that is possible to change this policy? Here in Spain the youth have responded magnificently by rallying 100,000 young volunteers, largely aged between 16 and 18, to the People's Army. They are coming forward to defend the future of their country and of World Democracy. We are proud to be fighting side by side with such a splendid body of youth.

But is it not a terrible tragedy that the flower of Spanish youth, the hope of the future should have to pass through the fires of war? Those of us who have come to Spain from the democratic countries feel a burning shame because of the irresponsibility of our Governments in permitting this war to be prolonged.

We are further convinced that a speedy victory of the Spanish Republic is necessary to save all the peoples from being plunged into fascist world war.

We therefore appeal to you, comrade, to act now! Let the youth in every country be the spearhead of a mighty People's movement for freedom and solidarity with the Spanish Republic. Sweep away all barriers and overwhelm the reactionary forces that are plotting your destruction.

Act now so as to save further suffering and loss of life in this war in Spain!

Act now so as to save the youth of the whole world from passing through the agony of war! Support us in this struggle and the speedy victory of Peace and Democracy throughout the world is certain!

DAVID GUEST,
(British Battalion. Killed in action during the recent Ebro offensive).

For more information see 'David Guest – A Scientist fights for freedom (1911–38)', a Memoir edited by Carmel Haden Guest. (Lawrence and Wishart 1939).

See also 'Open letter to the youth of all countries'. Appeal by David Guest. Written shortly before his death and published posthumously in, 'Volunteer for Liberty' September 5th, 1938

George Leeson

Along with other members of his company he was taken prisoner at the battle of Jarama in February 1937. In exchange for captured fascist officers these were released in May 1937. Leeson, and Morry Goldberg, who were both Jewish, were not freed until September 1937. This was undoubtedly the result of anti-Semitism. On his return to England Leeson was invited to speak at a meeting of the Battersea Trades Council about his experience in Franco's jails. See Battersea Trades Council, Minutes of sub-committee November 28th, 1937.

He later became active in the International Brigade Association and was a member of the Editorial Board of 'Volunteer for Liberty', the Brigade's journal. See 'Jarama Memories', and, 'May Day – A Symposium'. From 1953 until 1956 he was the General Manager of Unity Theatre..

Martin Messer

Originally from Glasgow he became a railway clerk and was a member of the Young Communist League. His connection with Battersea is not known. Trades Council delegates stood in silence on being notified of his death and letters of condolences were sent to his relatives.

Tom Oldershaw

At the time of his departure for Spain he lived at 74, Balham Park Road, SW12. The house was known as a 'Community House' and was shared with other Communist Party members. A carpenter by trade he was a member of the Battersea Number two branch of the Amalgamated Society of Woodworkers. Tom Oldershaw seconded the original motion to the Trades Council to establish an Aid to Spain committee. He was a member of the Aid to Spain sub-committee of the Trades Council, and its Secretary, from December 1936, until May 1937. He relinquished the post because he was, "no longer eligible to act as secretary", presumably this was because he was a member of the Communist Party. He left for Spain some time after this, in May/June 1937 and completed his training in November 1937.

Tom Oldershaw was a Political Commissar in the International Brigade. Commissar's were an integral part of the army with the job of inspiring their unit with discipline and loyalty. They worked in conjunction with the military

MODERN CRUSADERS

Battersea Lads in Spain

To the Editor.

SIR,—The following is a copy of a letter I have received from four Battersea members of the Saklatvala Battalion of the International Brigade. They all volunteered about a month ago and made their way to Spain. Each one felt it his duty to enlist in the services of the Spanish Government for democracy. All had lived in Battersea a considerable number of years, and Mr. Bert Sines was born in the borough.

I think that this letter will be of interest to the people of Battersea.

Yours etc.,
G. FINERAN.
177 Lavender Hill.
February 3, 1937.

The letter is as follows:—

Socorro Rojo,
Chamber 161,
Plaza Del Altozona,
Albacete, Spain.

DEAR COMRADES,—It is with great pride that we lads of the "Saklatvala Battalion," hear that you and the workers of Battersea are raising the necessary cash for a field ambulance. Comrades, all your efforts re the fight for democracy in Spain gives us all (Battersea lads especially) extra confidence.

Comrades, away with Fascism. Forward to our objectives in life. We, the undersigned, have seen with our own eyes that " Unity " and only " Unity " can ensure victory.

With our very best greetings to all Battersea people.—Yours fraternally,

BERT SINES (C.P.).
J. BROOMFIELD (No Party).
E. J. BEE (Labour Party).
G. W. BAKER (N.U.G.&M.W.).

The Battersea Ambulance for Spain fund has now reached nearly £200.

The following amounts have been received:—

	£	s.	d.
Collected at public meetings	119	5	6½
B.B.C. Departments	2	6	10
Trade Union branches	17	18	11
Co-op. organisations	4	5	9
Private subscribers	15	0	6
Labour Youth house-to-house collections	20	11	6
Labour Party	2	17	3
	£182	6	3½

South Western Star, 5th February, 1937.

commander, and were often elected He had been the Political Commissar for the Machine Gun Company. At the start of Franco's Aragon offensive he took over from Wally Tapsell as Political Commissar because Tapsell was on sick leave. Wounded in the advance from Caspe on March 16th, 1938, Tom Oldershaw was given first aid and left in a small archway. He was not there when a group returned to carry him to the rear, and he was never seen again. Political Commissars were usually shot by the Fascists.

It was wrongly announced at the Trades Council meeting of May 1938 that Tom Oldershaw had been captured. It is an indication of the lack of proper information that was being received in Britain about the fate of the volunteers (See Trades Council Minutes May 5th, 1938).

Bert Sines

One of the few of the volunteers to be born in Battersea, he lived at, 67, Bolingbroke Grove, near Wandsworth Common. He enlisted in the International Brigade at the beginning of 1937. See 'Modern Crusaders' Letter to 'South Western Star' February 5th, 1937.

He was invalided out of Brigade after being wounded, but returned to Spain in 1938. He spoke at the Teruel Victory celebration at the Town Hall in January, 1938. He was still in the International Brigade when it was demobilised by the Spanish Government in October 1938.

Very little is known about the following. More information would be most welcome.

G.W. Baker

The only G. Baker referred to in the International Brigade Archive was a Welsh miner, with no connections with Battersea. The sole reference is the letter to G. Fineran published in the South Western Star February 5th, 1937.

J. Broomfield

There is nothing referring to him in the International Brigade Archive. Again the sole reference is the letter to G. Fineran (Battersea Trades and Labour Council) from Spain. See, South Western Star February 5th, 1937.

Percy Cohen

He was the first driver of the Battersea Ambulance. He was referred to in the Minutes of the Trades Council Aid to Spain sub-committee, November 28th, 1937. In the Minutes the Spanish Medical Aid Committee stated that he was home on a few days leave, and was prepared to speak at meetings about Spain.

David Halloran

His name was inscribed on the banner carried by Battersea Communist Party to celebrate the 1937 May Day. It stated that he was one of six Battersea

Jarama Memories

Into Battle
By George Leeson

AFTER a few hours' sleep in full equipment on the concrete floor of a schoolhouse we mounted lorries in the early hours of morning. Day was just breaking when we tumbled out near a white house to the left of Morata de Tajuña. The front was about a mile and a half ahead and it was with the imminence of battle in our minds that we filed through the cookhouse to get the can of coffee and chunk of bread which was to be our food for the day.

We moved up to the line, dumped our packs, overcoats, and other impedimenta. Our pace quickened to the double as we heard the crackle of heavy rifle and machine-gun fire close ahead and stray bullets begain to whine through the trees.

It was the first time our British Battalion was going into action as a unit and the majority of the men were coming under fire for the first time in their lives.

My company had eight old Maxim guns, put together from a variety of spare parts, but no ammunition to fit them had arrived. We had to park them behind the line.

Already the battle for Pingarron Hill was raging and two of our companies were holding firm without cover. Casualties were piling up as the men were machine-gunned from the air and the ground, bombed, and shelled by the enemy artillery. Bill Briskey, a London busman, had fallen leading his company, and many another fine comrade gave his life.

The olive grove in which my section took up position was being riddled by fire which splintered the trees and lopped off twigs and branches. The Fascists could see us clearly and it was a case of holding on somehow and letting them have it every time they tried to advance.

I remember being with two other comrades behind one tree which an enemy machine-gunner decided was a likely point. Bursts of eight and ten rounds chipped the bark around the roots and tore into the light soil around us.

Young McKeown of Liverpool was determined to have a go and raised his head to take aim. He had not brought his rifle to his shoulder when a bullet caught him full in the temple and he fell on top of me, his blood streaming through the breast of my tunic and soaking me.

Many other incidents stand out in that terrific day. How we calmly and methodically mowed down the Moors every time they tried to rush us, yelling their blood-curdling war cries. A young Tyneside lad with a bullet through his knee and another through his ankle, in intense agony and calling for his father—he could not have been more than 18. The outstanding courage of Ralph Campean, Commissar of No. 1 Company, refusing to leave the line though mortally wounded. Jimmy Prendergast in his shirt sleeves rallying a group of some five survivors: "Keep it up, we'll hold the bastards."

The biggest impression I have of the battle is the indomitable courage and determination of our comrades, their Cockney, Tyneside, Scots, Irish, and many other brands of humour which made the most dangerous moments seem as nothing.

MAY DAY
A SYMPOSIUM

Talavera (G. Leeson)

I SPENT May Day, 1937, in a prison at Talavera de la Reina. The prison was called "Tinajos," and was actually a filthy disused factory which had once been used to manufacture "tinajos" (large earthenware wine jars), and was a clearing house for prisoners brought from the front or the surrounding villages. New prisoners arrived almost daily, and there was a regular passage of prisoners out, some to other prisons, some to serve in Franco's labour battalions, and a regular stream to face the firing squad at the cemetery just along the road.

There was usually about three hundred prisoners in Tinajos, including about forty International Brigaders; British, French, German, Belgian, Hungarian, Polish, Danish, and Czech.

Life was far from pleasant for us. The threat of death hung over the prison, made more vivid by the arrival once or twice daily of the "death wagon," the van which carried prisoners to execution. We were taken on work parties to the cemetery where the executions took place and where a foul pit was used as a common grave for our valiant comrades, who faced death as only the workers can. We had no bedding, but slept on the ground, no clean clothes, only the rags of our uniforms, we had no facilities for washing and the whole place was infested with lice. The front was only about ten miles away, and the town swarmed with Moors, who continually threatened to butcher all of us should the Republican troops advance nearer the town.

On May Day, there was a tense keyed-up feeling among the prisoners and the guards were careful to avoid provoking any of us. The papers were filled with plans for Franco's festival of the Spanish race which was to take place the next day. News of the Italian defeat at Guadalajara began to trickle through, and we gathered in groups to talk about May Day to re-affirm our will to fight for the international brotherhood of mankind and our confidence in the victory of the Republic.

No executions took place that day, and no work parties were sent out. Our principal celebration was the visit of a Republican plane which flew over the town and bombed the railway track.

In the evening we gathered together and sang songs of all countries, a regular evening performance, but carried through with much more seriousness and gusto than usual.

May Day lives in the hearts of the workers of all lands. Prisons, setbacks and the threat of death can never extinguish it. Prisoners in Franco's camps will greet each other with the clenched fist salute this May Day just as we did on May 1, 1937.

men who had gone to fight Franco. See, South Western Star May 7th, 1937. His name was also included on the roll of honour of the Battersea men killed in Spain. See Report of the Memorial Meeting for David Guest and Tom Oldershaw, South Western Star September 9th, 1938

Joe Ilean

He was referred to as, "the driver of the Battersea Ambulance" See South Western Star December 16th, 1938. Presumably he drove the ambulance after Cohen.

Michael Kelly

His name was also inscribed on the banner carried by the Battersea Communist Party to celebrate the 1937 May Day (see above). Name also included on roll of honour of Battersea men killed in Spain (see above).

The Aid to Spain Movement in Battersea

The transcript of a talk given by Noreen Branson to the Wandsworth History Workshop, on May 12th, 1992.

Before I start, I think I ought to say that my husband Clive and I lived in Glycena Road, which is a turning off of Lavender Hill. He was an artist, but at the time he was working in the Education Department of the Communist Party, at 16, King Street. He also did a lot of lecturing for the National Council of Labour Colleges. When the Spanish War started, in July 1936, I was the secretary of the Battersea branch of the Communist Party. I held this position, not because I was a very leading activist, but because I could type, that was probably the reason. Battersea in those days was a very different place to what it is today. It was a highly industrialised part of the world and there were engineering factories everywhere. The Communist Party branch had about 50 members. We had members who worked in Dorman Longs engineering works, Morgan Crucible engineering works, Battersea Bus Garage, and the Rail Depot at Nine Elms. There were also some members over the border, working in the Projectile engineering works. Those are the places I can actually remember. I also remember Prices Candle factory which used to smell so dreadfully on certain occasions.

We soon realised that North Battersea was a solid Labour constituency and South Battersea was not, it was sort of half and half, and at that time I think it did not have a Labour MP. I think I should remind you that what was so awful about the Spanish War was that the Government decided on a non-intervention policy, which meant that the Spanish Government was forbidden to buy arms to defend itself against General Franco's assault. While at the same time, General Franco had troops and aircraft and arms of all kinds flooding in from Hitler Germany and fascist Italy. He was being supported by the fascist powers and here our Government refused to allow the Spanish Government to buy arms to defend itself, and actually got the agreement of France, and other European countries, that they also should ban arms sales to the Spanish Republican Government.

The first thing that the Battersea branch of the Communist Party did was to organise a series of public meetings on this question of non-intervention.

The first one took place on the 31st of July, under the slogan, 'Support Spanish Workers against Fascism'. It was held in the Unity Hall, Falcon Grove. I don't remember much about that meeting, although I do remember much clearer the second one we held, which was on September 13th at Battersea Town Hall. The speakers included Johnny Campbell, and Ted Bramley, who was the District Secretary of the Communist Party. The local speakers were my husband Clive, and Dan Lewis, who was the local CP organiser for S.W. London. He was in our branch and he made the collection. Four hundred people turned up to the meeting, and we made a collection of £13.10d, which was quite a lot in those days. The average wage was about three pounds a week for a male manual worker, and a good deal less for women workers. On October 10th, we held another anti fascist meeting, and this was right in the middle of what came to be known as the Battle of Cable Street, and we were all acutely aware of the need to protect ourselves from fascism.

In the meantime great anger was building up against the non-intervention policy, and in particular against the fact that the Labour Party and the TUC had both decided to support the non-intervention policy. Some broad national committees had been set up, particularly one for Medical Aid for Spain, in which doctors and nurses were participating, and money was being raised to send ambulances. We booked the Town Hall for November 1st, and we asked Isabel Brown to come and speak. Isabel Brown was one of the greatest orators I have ever known, and she was one of the inauguraters of the Spanish Medical Aid Committee nationally. We also asked the Labour MP Aneurin Bevan whether he would speak, because he was against the non-intervention policy. He said he would like to speak, but it would be easier if the meeting was not called under the auspices of the Communist Party. We could understand that because there was a great deal of witch hunting going on at that time against communists. So we agreed to this, and the meeting was advertised as an Aid to Spain event. It was absolutely packed out. I don't know how many people the Town Hall held in those days, but there must have been something like a thousand people there. We collected over £40, which would be like collecting two thousand pounds today. It was an incredible event. We had also decided that what we ought to do was to aim for the setting up of a broad Aid to Spain Committee in Battersea, and that these meetings should stop just being called by the Communist Party. We discussed this with some of our members who were delegates to the Battersea Trades Council from their local trade union branches. Among those involved in this were David Guest and Tom Oldershaw. David Guest had been a prominent left wing activist in the student movement, and had come to Battersea and set up a People's Bookshop on

Lavender Hill, at number 115. The object of it was to sell left wing books. The rooms over the top of the shop were used as meeting places, not only for the Communist Party but also for other organisations, particularly the NUWM, the Unemployed Workers Movement, and also for the Left Book Club. Although David Guest was running the Bookshop, the main person working there was Wally Pritchard, who had been a meat porter at Smithfield Market.

David and his colleague both joined the Shop Assistants Union and David became the delegate to the Battersea Trades Council. Tom Oldershaw was a carpenter, and he was already a delegate to the Trades Council. They proposed that the Trades Council should set up the Battersea Aid Spain Committee. At the Council's November 1936 meeting this was agreed to. It was agreed that it should be a broad committee, not just confined to trade union branches, but should include other organisations.

From then on I attended the Battersea Aid Spain Committee meetings as a delegate from the North Battersea Women's Co-operative Guild . After the committee's formation, the Battersea Communist Party handed over the £40 that we had collected from our meeting on November 1st. The Aid Spain Committee met regularly from then on at 177, Lavender Hill, which was the HQ of the local Labour Party .

The first thing the Committee decided to do was to hold what was called a Spain Week. The Spain Week was held from December 6th–13th. Every organisation was asked to make whatever contribution they could. Outstanding among the activities was the collection of food for the Spanish Youth Food ship. This was a national campaign which had been launched by John Gollan, who was the leader of the Young Communist League, and Ted Willis, who was leader of the Labour League of Youth. Ted Willis became the secretary of the National Committee.

In Battersea, members of the Young Communist League and the Labour League of Youth leafleted streets, asking for a tin of milk or a pound of sugar, or a tin of any other kind of food. In those days very few people had refrigerators, and although people had milk delivered it had to be drunk very quickly before it went off. So everyone had lots of tins of milk as a back up, some people only had tinned milk. Streets were leafleted asking for food or milk, and then the young people went around pushing wheelbarrows to collect the food. The response was absolutely incredible. We aimed to collect a ton of food, and according to our estimates it would need five thousand tins of milk to make a ton of food. By the end of the week they had collected three quarters of a ton, and were determined to collect a ton before Christmas. When the food ship sailed out on Christmas eve, with a cargo of ninety three tons, we claimed that one ton had come from Battersea. This was probably true. It was ready to sail from Southampton on Christmas Eve, and Southampton dockers, who loaded it, gave their pay towards the collection for the next food ship.

Other things also happened during the Spain Week. It included knitting for Spain. Sixty garments were knitted by women who sat in the front of the window of the People's Bookshop. We did a lot of collecting at various workplaces. Some of the best collections were at the Battersea Bus Garage. We also sang Christmas carols in aid for Spain.

Spain Week ended with another Town Hall meeting on the 13th of December, which was called by the Aid Spain committee. Twenty organisations were officially represented on the platform. These consisted of eight TU branches, two Women's Co-op Guilds, a local Tenants Association, five Labour Party wards, two Labour League of Youth branches, the Battersea Communist Party, and the Battersea YCL. Those were the organisations represented on the platform, although there were more affiliates than that on the Aid to Spain committee. The Town Hall was again packed, and a collection of £55 was made. Among the speakers was the local MP, Stephen Sanders, and also the scientific correspondent of the 'News Chronicle', Langdon Davis. He told the meeting that if we didn't defeat fascism in Spain, we and France would be the next countries under threat. Save London Save Madrid, became the slogan of the movement. Councillor Fineran, who was the secretary of the Battersea Borough Labour Party, reported on the activities of the Aid to Spain Committee, and the meeting was chaired by Clive Branson.

After Christmas activities didn't end with the Aid Spain week, they continued on into 1937. Early in January the committee launched a campaign to raise money for an ambulance to go to Spain. £200, which had been collected earlier, was sent to the national Medical Aid Committee to which it was suggested that an ambulance should be sent out in the name of Battersea. This was agreed, and we continued collecting money until we had reached seven hundred and fifty pounds, which was the amount needed for the ambulance. After that an ambulance was sent to Spain with Battersea written on the side.

There were a innumerable meetings and events on behalf of Spain. At the People's Bookshop, over the window, Clive drew a huge map of the road from London to Madrid and stuck it up on great placard, and we got a toy ambulance and moved it along another section every time we raised fifty pounds.

What I remember best was what my North Battersea Co-op Guild did. We staged an event which included a bazaar, a children's tea party, and ended with a carnival dance and a Spanish cabaret. It was held on the 23rd February 1937. We discussed all this at my Guild meeting at great length, and one of the members of the Guild, Mrs Varran, got up and said she thought we ought to ask Mrs Saklatvala to open this bazaar. Much to my surprise this was unanimously agreed, and everybody was enthusiastic at the idea. Saklatvala had died in January 1936, and hadn't been the MP in Battersea North since 1929. There were a lot of people around in Battersea who we called the Saklatvalaites, and Mrs Varran was one of them. The point was, she explained to me, that the Labour Party to which she had belonged had been dissolved, and another one had been set up by Labour Party HQ, and she had refused to join it. That was the case with several other people.

We got out posters for the bazaar, and I went with Mrs Varran down to Battersea High Street market, to ask the stall holders if they would hang them up. The first stall we went to, Mrs Varran went up with a poster and said to the stall holder would he mind putting up a poster which advertised an Aid Spain bazaar. The stall holder looked at us rather doubtfully, and then he saw the name Mrs Saklatvala, and he said, "Mrs Saklatvala, I'd do anything for her" and put the poster up. I was rather surprised, but this was a fairly typical reaction; obviously it was very good publicity. Mrs Saklatvala was a widow, and was the wife of an MP who had been much loved. It was a very good thing to have Mrs Saklatvala's name on this poster, because it attracted a lot of people.

The bazaar was followed by a children's tea-party. All the children who came to this party were told to bring a bag with no less than two pennies in it. The bags they brought had far more than two pennies – indeed we made quite a lot of money from them. The bags were handed over to one of our helpers who was dressed as a fairy and had with her my little daughter, aged four, and another little girl from Glycena Road aged six, both of whom were also dressed as fairies. The children then sat down to have tea and eat the cakes which had been made by the Co-op guilds-women. There was also an all night dance which went on in the evening, and everyone paid sixpence for their entry, and it made a great deal of money. I don't know how much as I haven't kept a record.

Another example of what was going on was the Music Group. It was organised by somebody called Denzil Dix. Denzil Dix was a pianist, who couldn't sight read, but played entirely by ear. Because Arding and Hobbs, the Department Store, sold pianos, they employed him to sit in their window and play the piano for a couple of hours very day. That was his job. His wife, Naomi Dix, was a singing teacher. They organised a large number of events for Spain. The most outstanding one was at the end of 1937, when they staged a music competition concert, and there were thirty eight competitors. Everybody came to it, and a councillor called Wye, who was an active member of the Aid Spain Committee, presided. By the end of this time the full £750 was raised for the ambulance.

Sometime in 1937 instructions came down from Fineran, who was secretary of the Borough Labour Party, that the Communist Party must not be represented on the Battersea Aid Spain Committee, because it was against the Labour Party rules. We had a long discussion about this on the Communist Party branch committee. We decided that in the interests of the movement we would withdraw our official representative, but the rest of us went on attending because we were representing other organisations. The chairman of the Aid Spain Committee, who was Councillor Coles, and whom I greatly admired, turned a blind eye to all this, so we continued to participate in the Committee. The secretary of the Aid Spain Committee was somebody called Ned Skinner, and I think he worked at Morgan Crucibles .

From 1937 onwards a major concentration was for the Dependents Aid Committee, which had been set up to help the families of those who had gone to fight in Spain. The first person who went from Battersea to fight in Spain was somebody called Bert Sines. He was an engineer, who I knew very well. He had fought in the First World War, and had experience as a gunner. He was wounded and came back, and then went back again. There were three others who went to fight in Spain . One was Clive Branson, another was David Guest, who was killed, and another was Tom Oldershaw, who was a carpenter who had been on the Aid Spain committee, he too was killed. I can't remember the names of the other people who went from Battersea to fight, although there were one or two.

I'll go into some detail about what happened to my husband Clive. Clive thought he ought to go and fight in Spain. When he suggested it, Harry Pollitt said no, he wanted him to stay in England. Early in 1937 it was made illegal for people to go to Spain, or to be recruited to go to Spain. So all the volunteers that had been turning up at 16, King Street, the CP HQ, to volunteer, were told that on no account must they go near King Street. Clive was one of the people who established the organisation for coping with this. A sandwich bar was set up not far from 16, King Street, where all the people who wanted to volunteer were told to go and report to the man behind the bar. He would then contact Clive, who would then contact the volunteers.

Clive also acted as the courier who took the groups to Paris and handed them over. Most of the people who went, went on weekend visiting tickets, that way you didn't need a passport. Clive had a passport and he use to go and take them and come back again. He didn't communicate with the volunteers until they were on the ship. Once, when he was at Victoria Station, a train driver who knew Clive, waved at him and gave the Red Front salute. The police were standing there by the barrier looking at people who were going, because they were already very suspicious. Clive turned his back and pretended not to know the train driver. After he had been doing this for nearly a year the police began to get on to him, so it was agreed that the job should be handed over to somebody else.

In January 1938, Clive went to Spain, and was captured in April. The interesting thing was, that although I never saw anything of the police supervision until after Clive had gone, two days after his departure I noticed that there were three men standing in front of the house opposite all day, watching who was going in and out of our door. It was clear that they had lost track of the person who they thought was doing this job, and knowing where he lived, had come to see what had happened. I was rather entertained by all this I must admit, as they had obviously come too late.

After Clive went to Spain I ceased to be the secretary of the Communist Party branch, because I went to work part time for the Labour Research Department. After 1938 I didn't participate in the work of the branch to anything like the extent that I had done previously. I haven't got much of a record of the events in Battersea for 1938 because of that – but the campaign for Spain went on.

In November 1938, Clive came back. He had been captured and was released as part of an exchange for Italian prisoners. In December, I think, the rest of the International Brigade came back. After they'd come back we still went on demanding arms for Spain, and there was a call to join a march for arms for Spain sometime in January or February 1939, in London. The workers at Dorman Longs downed tools at four o'clock and went and joined the demonstration, and they were one of the biggest contingents. So we were rather proud of that. I have to say that in March, when the Spanish Government was finally forced to surrender, and Franco won, it was one of the most awful things that any of us ever experienced. We had done all this fighting, but had been completely defeated. And of course, as you pointed out, it was one of the reasons why we had a war. The point was, that all this helping Franco by our Government, was something that in the end led to the Second World War, without any question.

Notes

1. Nan Green and A.M. Elliot, *Spain against Fascism 1936–39*. Our History Pamphlet No 67. Published by Communist Party History Group, 1976.
2. *South Western Star*, August 7th, 1936.
3. Ibid.
4. *South Western Star*, August 21st, 1936.
5. See *Noreen Branson reminiscences*, in this pamphlet.
6. *South Western Star*, November 6th, 1936.
7. See *Noreen Branson reminiscences*.
8. *Battersea Trades Council Minutes*, Thursday November 4th, 1936, at the Board Room, Latchmere Baths.
9. *Battersea Trades Council Minutes*, December 3rd, 1936.
10. *Battersea Trades Council. Aid to Spain Sub Committee*, November 29th, 1936. Hereafter referred to as Trades Council Sub-Committee.
11. *Noreen Branson*, and *South Western Star*, December 4th, 1936.
12. *David Guest – A Scientist Fights for Freedom (1911–1938) A Memoir*. Edited by Carmel Hayden Guest. Contribution from Councillor Wye. (Lawrence and Wishart 1939).
13. *South Western Star*, January 8th and 15th, 1937.
14. *David Guest – A Scientist Fights for Freedom*. Contribution from Councillor Wye.
15. *Trades Council Sub Committee*, June 28th, 1937.
16. *Trades Council Minutes*, May 5th, 1938.
17. *South Western Star*, July 15th, 1938.
18. *Trades Council, Minutes of Sub Committee*, November 28th, 1937.
19. *South Western Star*, February 19th, 1937.
20. *South Western Star*, January 22nd, 1937.
21. *South Western Star*, February 12th, 1937.
22. See Chris Wrigley, *Battersea Republicans and the 1902 Coronation*, Battersea and Wandsworth Labour and Social History Group.
23. *South Western Star*, April 2nd, 1937.
24. *South Western Star*, February 26th, 1937.
25. *South Western Star*, October 28th, 1938.
26. *South Western Star*, January 14th, 1938.
27. A large number of children from the Basque region of Spain were evacuated to Britain after Franco's attack on the area.
28. *Battersea Trades Council Minutes*, September 1st, 1938.
29. *South Western Star*, January 6th, 1939, and *Trades Council Minutes and Sub Committee Minutes*, August–January, 1939.
30. *Battersea Trades Council Minutes*, December 1st, 1938.
31. *South Western Star*, February 3rd, 1939.
32. *South Western Star*, January 27th, 1939.
33. *South Western Star*, February 3rd, 1939.
34. *Battersea Trades Council Minutes*, July 6th, 1939.
35. *Battersea Trades Council Minutes*, October 4th, 1939.

36 *South Western Star*, September 25th, 1936.
37 *South Western Star*, February 25th, 1938.
38 *South Western Star*, April 29th, 1938.
39 *South Western Star*, July 15th, 1938. There are no references to the activities of the Peace Council in the local paper, usually a good source, after July 1938.
40 *South Western Star*, June 18th, 1937.
41 *South Western Star*, July 9th, 1937.
42 *South Western Star*, February 11th, 1938.
43 *South Western Star*, February 3rd, 1939.
44 David Guest, Letter to YCL comrade, in *A Scientist Fights for Freedom*.
45 *South Western Star*, March 10th, 1939.
46 *Battersea Trades Council Minutes*, 6th, May, 1937.
47 *Labour Party 37th Annual Conference Report*, 1937.
48 See *Noreen Branson reminiscences*.
49 *South Western Star*, May 7th, 1937.
50 *South Western Star*, November 12th, 1937.
51 *South Western Star*, September 9th, 1938.
52 *South Western Star*, January 15th, 1937.
53 *Daily Worker*, June 7th, 1933.
54 *Daily Worker*, July 1st, 1933.
55 See *Evening Standard*, November 9th, 1933 and *Daily Sketch*, November 10th, 1933.
56 *Daily Worker*, February 13th, 1934.
57 *South Western Star*, October 16th, 1936.
58 *South Western Star*, March 18th, 1938.
59 *South Western Star*, April 1st, 1938.
60 *South Western Star*, April 8th, 1938.
61 *South Western Star*, February 10th, 1939.
62 *South Western Star*, April 21st, 1939.
63 John Mahon, *Harry Pollitt: A Biography*. (Lawrence and Wishart, p.242).
64 David Guest – *A Scientist Fights for Freedom*. Contribution from Councillor Wye, and *South Western Star*, September 9th, 1938.